A GUIDE TO EMPOWERMENT, REVOLUTION, AND THE UNIVERSAL RIGHT TO BE FREE

A FUTURE TO BELIEVE IN

108 REFLECTIONS ON THE ART AND ACTIVISM OF FREEDOM

"There is a tendency to think that what we see in the present moment will continue. We forget how often we have been astonished by the sudden crumbling of institutions, by extraordinary changes in people's thoughts, by unexpected eruptions of rebellion against tyrannies, by the quick collapse of systems of power that seemed invincible."

~ Howard Zinn

World Dharma Publications
2768 West Broadway
Post Office Box 74709
Vancouver, B.C., Canada V6K 2G4

Cover design by World Dharma Publications
Typography by World Dharma Publications

Library of Congress Cataloging-in-Publication Data
Clements, Alan 1951 —

A FUTURE TO BELIEVE IN
108 REFLECTIONS ON THE ART AND ACTIVISM OF FREEDOM

Alan Clements
p. cm.
ISBN-13: 978-0615521428 (alk. Paper)

1. Liberty — freedom — Buddhism 2. Spiritual life — Buddhism — non-sectarian 3. Human rights — all aspects 4. Social, Political and Environmental justice — all 5. Activism — all 6. Consciousness — all 7. Politics — global 8. Body, Mind & Spirit
BQ7657. F7 C87 2009
292. 3 777 — August 20   2009 2011 807

First printing, August 31, 2011
ISBN-13: 978-0615521428
Printed in USA on acid-free, recycled paper

10 9 8 7 6 5 4 3 2

Praise for **A FUTURE TO BELIEVE IN**

"This culture is killing the planet. If we are to have any future at all, we must unlearn everything this culture has taught us and begin to listen to the planet, to listen to life — the core intelligence of nature and the human heart. This book not only helps us with that unlearning process — the greatest challenge humankind has every faced — it provides the essential wisdom, the spiritual intelligence, to open ourselves to finally start to hear."

~ **Derrick Jensen, Author of** *Endgame* **and** *Deep Green Resistance*

"This book is the music of wisdom, a dance with the finest places of the human heart. It is also like a walk with your favorite friends, mentors and teachers as they point out the beauties of the journey. You will want to keep this timeless treasure within reach, so you can open it to any page, and let a paragraph or a line ignite you again to the truth of your own being."

~ **Joanna Macy, Author of** *World as Lover, World As Self* **and** *Pass it On: Five Stories that Can Change the World*

"For 10,000 years, the mantra of our material civilization has been *Compete and Consume*, but the inspiration for the new paradigm is to *Cooperate and Conserve*. Alan Clements' elegant, humane Reflections teach us how to cooperate in order to cherish and preserve that good and beautiful and raptured thing we call freedom. Achieving that is the key to building a future that loves and protects the biosphere within which we interdepend. This is a wonderful collection of wise and glittering things that will travel everywhere from hand to hand, and heart to heart."

~ **Gregory David Roberts, Author of** *Shantaram*

"At a time when the contemporary spiritual landscape has become dangerously gentrified and domesticated, Alan Clements restores us to our senses — wild and elemental. He summons the voices of those who, along side him, have not traded their souls for the market-driven need to be tame or acceptable, and points us to the wilderness of true, engaged, fiercely authentic awakening. This is why we are alive — to set freedom free, in ourselves and for others, in every aspect of our lives from the most mundane daily task, to the most profound political act."

~ **Kelly Wendorf, Author and editor** *Stories of Belonging*

A Future To Believe In provides us with a standing wave of insight, a perpetually central pivot pertaining eminently to private and political spheres, inextricable, afterall. This book should be made mandatory world-wide for all heads of state."

~ **Lissa Wolsak, Author of** *In Defense of Being, Squeezed Light* **and** *Pen Chants*

"*A Future To Believe In* is a book that carries the necessary tension to encourage and motivate the critical self reflection so necessary for the healing and transformation so desperately needed in the world."

~ **Claude AnShin Thomas, Award winning author of** *At Hell's Gate: A Soldier's Journey From War To Peace. Zen Buddhist Monk* **and** *Vietnam Combat Veteran*

"Radical wisdom, from a revolutionary spirit. These reflections inspired me to be kind, compassionate and unflinching in the face of suffering and ignorance. This is a field guide for spiritual revolutionaries, a manifesto of liberation. If you care about anything, read this book."

~ **Noah Levine, Author of** *Dharma Punx* **and** *Against the Stream*

"*A Future to Believe In* is rich feast of wisdom best taken in small bites, calling us to the highest and best within each of us — to a life of integrity, perspective, and compassion."

~ **Dan Millman, Author of** *Way of the Peaceful Warrior* **and** *The Four Purposes of Life*

"This surprising collection of aphorisms, reflections, and anecdotes is a rare thing: both a deep source for inner renewal as well as a manual for changing ourselves and the world around us."

~ Stephen Batchelor, Author of *Buddhism without Beliefs*

"Alan Clements has put together an enchanting treasury of *dharma* jewels — inspired reflections and compassionate insights on life and freedom — in the cosmos, on Earth, in human society and above all in the human heart. The short pieces in this book will be cherished and savored for their soul-stirring beauty."

~ Ralph Metzner, Ph.D., Author of *MindSpace* and *TimeStream*

"In this radiant book is an orchard — trees of wise ripe fruits, where you may stroll, gathering such fulfilled thoughts and emotions...to savor each' flavor, aroma, ambience — to then contemplate within this luxuriant garden a new consciousness and, thereby, chose, pick — strike forth — and act with such sure support to shape a future to believe in."

~ Lowry Burgess, Artist and professor at Carnegie Mellon — creator of the first official Non-Scientific Art Payload taken into outer space by NASA in 1989; also author of the 2001 *Toronto Manifesto, The Right to Human Memory*

"Alan Clements once again offers words that shift our attention away from the too easy to identity sordid events of the world and toward the heartbeat that enlivens the spirit in all of us, a spirit that yearns for discovery, growth, and peace. *A Future to Believe In* will inspire readers to reflect on the personal philosophies that shape their thoughts and then, most importantly, subtly nudge them into some new caring and creative course of action."

~ Dr. Sam Richards, professor of sociology and co-director of the World in Conversation Project at Penn State University

"*A Future to Believe* is a tapestry of wisdom and inspiration from countless cultures and eras of humanity."

~ Eunice Wong, Essayist and Books Editor at Truthdig

"Alan Clements' book is well-timed, in that, most people in our world have lost hope for the future. I am confident that *"A Future to Believe In"* will rekindle in their minds a new vision — inspiring all to listen fully to their own hearts, and learn to understand the universal laws of Nature that govern us — that make life and Cosmos the miracle of love that it is. Please spread this book far and wide."

~ **Dr. A.T.Ariyaratne, Founder of Sarvodaya Movement of Sri Lanka.**

"Drawing on a wonderful blend of artists, poets and teachers, activists, scientists, and sages, Alan Clements offers us reflections that call forth our hearts. They invite a dedication to creating a peaceful, vibrant, beautiful world — one that honors the sanctity of freedom, dignity, and human rights."

~ **Tara Brach, Author, *Radical Acceptance***

"This brilliant almanac of wisdom for everyday life is a must-read for anyone seeking inspiration, and spiritual know-how, in these challenging times. I've never read anything quite like *"A Future To Believe In."* Absolutely wonderful."

~ **Mark Matousek, Author of *Ethical Wisdom: What Makes Us Good* and *When You're Falling, Dive: Lessons in the Art of Living***

"I value this book enormously. It is packed with transformative insight, compelling ideas, and remarkable articulations about the nature of being — who we are and what we can become. Rather than expecting us to embrace some bright belief in a path to enlightenment or peace, it ignites in us the passion of adventure and the courage to keep an open mind — free of conclusions — as we explore deep personal, social, and planetary transformation. I hope this book serves as a catalyst for both political activists and spiritual aspirants to keep alive the questioning mind, and further, a manual for contemplations and conversations to co-create newly true communities of deepening, committed, powerful people."

~ **Tom Atlee, Author of *The Tao of Democracy* and *Reflections on Evolutionary Activism* and founder of the Co-Intelligence Institute**

"Clements ranges far and deeply through the world's thinkers, mystics, activists, and poets to create a tapestry of challenge and encouragement — encouragement by showing that others have gone before us, and a challenge to go further, that the universe is waiting for our own contribution to the eternal process of liberation and fulfillment."

~ Dale Pendell, Author of *Pharmako/Gnosis, Plant Teachers and the Poison Path*, and *The Great Bay, Chronicles of the Collapse*

"We live in times that spread greed, violence, fear and hopelessness. We live in times when consumerism enslaves us while offering pseudo-freedom. Alan Clements labor of love, *"A Future to Believe In: A Guide to Revolution, Environmental Sanity, and the Universal Right to Be Free,"* brings us reflections that inspire us to be free and fearless."

~ Dr. Vandana Shiva, Author of, *Earth Democracy; Justice, Sustainability, and Peace, Soil, Not Oil*, and *Staying Alive.*

"This book is an act of spiritual activism. It comes to us from the frontline of the revolution in consciousness underway in the world today. It is a gift of wisdom that awakens us to the changes we need to make, but always seen from a spiritual perspective. Buy it as a daily reminder that will lift your awareness towards a better future."

~ Hardin Tibbs, Futurist and writer on industrial ecology, sustainability, cultural values, change, and other future-focused topics.

"Distilling the essence of world religions, cultures, politics, and spiritual traditions, Alan Clements' magnificent, timely book provides a courageous and intelligent compass personifying our aspirations for freedom and wisdom, and in so doing, offers insights on how to actively shape a future that gives life hope. With our planet in peril, it is imperative that we act now to provide a secure future for our children and future generations; make this book your guide, mentor and friend."

~ Dr Helen Caldicott, Author of *Nuclear Power is Not the Answer* and *If you Love this Planet;* Founding President Physicians for Social Responsibility.

FOR **Sahra**

"i carry your heart (i carry it in my heart)."

e.e. cummings

TABLE OF CONTENTS

A FUTURE TO BELIEVE IN
108 REFLECTIONS ON THE ART AND ACTIVISM OF FREEDOM

REFLECTION

REFLECTION

REFLECTION

REFLECTION

VISION

"I see children, all children, as humanity's most precious resource; because it will be to them that the care of the planet will always be left. One child must never be set above another, even in casual conversation, not to mention in speeches that circle the globe. As adults, we must affirm, constantly, that the Arab child, the Muslim child, the Palestinian child, the African child, the Jewish child, the Christian child, the American child, the Chinese child, the Israeli child, the Native American child, etc., is equal to all others on the planet. We must do everything in our power to cease the behavior that makes children everywhere feel afraid."

~ Alice Walker

INTRODUCTION

A Future to Believe In was created to be a timeless companion; opened anytime, anywhere, to read a reflection or two at a time. And left out, returned to, for insight and inspiration — a guide for empowerment, nonviolent revolution, environmental sanity, creative self-expression, and the universal right to be free.

1.   A FUTURE TO BELIEVE IN

"We are star stuff which has taken its destiny into its own hands."

~ Carl Sagan

*L*ife as we know it appears to be an isolated phenomenon confined to the surface of Earth, where we thrive within only a tiny bandwidth of refracted light. Alpha Centauri — the next nearest source of luminosity to our sun — is a star system twenty-five trillion miles away. This is but one of the four-hundred billion stars in our Milky Way Galaxy. And this is but one of the millions of billions of other galaxies in just our region of the cosmos, each containing countless stars. Reason dictates that the conditions for life exist elsewhere, but contacting that life, if it does exist, seems to be outside our current sphere of possibility. For all practical purposes we are an isolated colony spinning through eternity at six-thousand miles per hour.

"We don't want to know what the word *life* means to us," states Carol Cleland, philosopher in residence with NASA's National Astrobiology Institute. "We want to know what life *is*."

Max Planck, Nobel Prize-winning father of Quantum Theory, states: "All matter exists only by virtue of a force. We must assume behind this force the existence of a conscious and intelligent Mind... [And this] mind is the matrix of all matter."

Life is a precious opportunity.
But it is not enough to stand in awe of totality.

We must participate in the evolution of the intelligence in which we are embedded. The time for hope is over. We are in an era of actualization creating a future to believe in. There is knowledge and there is application of that knowledge. We all have a good sense of what we must do.

"The future of mankind lies waiting for those who will come to understand their lives and take up their responsibility to all living things."

~ **Vine Deloria Jr., American Indian author and activist.**

The point now is to embody this realization and act on behalf of the greater good — the interrelated whole, everybody, ourselves, one and the same.

Buckminster Fuller, the legendary architect, philosopher, and visionary, once said: "People say to me, I wonder what it would be like to be on a spaceship. And I [always respond in the same way]: you don't really realize what you are asking, because everybody is an Astronaut. We all live aboard a beautiful little spaceship called Earth. And if the success or failure of this planet and of human beings depended on how I am and what I do:

How would I be? What would I do?"

"I always tell people to have the highest aspirations."

~ **Aung San Suu Kyi**

Okay.

How would I be?

What will I do?

2.   TO DREAM

"We only become what we are by the radical and deep-seated refusal of that which others have made of us."

~ **Jean-Paul Sartre**

A political prisoner once described his jail cell to me. It had no windows. No bed. No toilet. No light. He lived for six months, naked, in a black box with the keyhole as the only ventilation. He told me that he survived by using his imagination — his ability to dream and think out of the box — the box of his own mind as much as the prison walls surrounding him.

He said he started by thinking out beyond his anger, his outrage, and fear. He began to think about the nature of the human psyche, which he saw as a complex network of conditioned imprints.

He began to think about the nature of those imprints and as he did he reflected on the nature of propaganda, mind control, and indoctrination.

He began to think about how nothing stands on its own — how everything is interdependent, arising from conditions. He also thought about how conditions are preceded by other conditions, and so on, *ad infinitum*.

Life was, he concluded, a beginningless, immeasurable inheritance of interrelated constituents, where everything is related in every way.

It was here — with a deeper, more nuanced appreciation for mutual-causality — that he felt forgiveness for his captors. They were, he reasoned, tragic victims of a particular programming. They were largely puppets, unaware, indoctrinated in denigrating structures inherited from a primordial legacy. This insight, he said, brought him some degree of compassion and joy and allowed him to dream more fully, with greater daring.

As a physicist he had some training in 'out of the box' thinking. He began to contemplate beyond this world, imagining the greater context — a universe without circumference.

Further, he began to imagine other life forms and other dimensions in this vastness. He explained that he became so enraptured using his imagination that after a while it turned to bliss. "I know it sounds strange," he concluded with an ironic grin. "I learned how to be happy, not through meditation or day-to-day life, but from my ability to dream within the confinement of my black box."

I ask myself, can I dream like this today?

Everyday?

Right now?

"Think of all the beauty still left around you and be happy."

~ Anne Frank

3. ENTER THE ADVENTURE

"Consciousness is the phenomenon whereby the universe's
very existence is made known."

~ Roger Penrose

*O*uter *life* — as seen through the senses and the circuitry
of perception — is a hyperspatial vibrancy of interlocking
energy patterns. A human face is one such pattern, as is
making love. But whose face is it, and who is making love
with whom? Physicists tell us that beneath visual life, beneath
how we ordinarily perceive things, lies a shimmering sea of
subatomic waves and particles and humans are holographic-
like excitations consisting of those very same energies.

Universal intelligence may be so multidimensional that life as
we know it may be the cinematic-like expression of a single
molecule of DNA; a God molecule of infinite complexity
among countless other such molecules within a Being — an
entity, a form of life we have no knowledge of.

"Science is not a formal logic," states Max Born,
Nobel laureate in Physics, "it needs the free play of the mind in
as great a degree as any other creative art."

Or maybe we're so microscopic that our infinity is a single cell
in the cerebral cortex of a creature crawling along a galactic
corridor in some world system — an organism imprinted
with the memory of the evolutionary code of consciousness,
while cognitively blind to the greater context of its existence,
the infinite universe.

It's possible. Of course, anything is.

That's Life — an unfathomable sea of potentialities: a magnificent and maddening blend of intelligence that bleeds, weeps, and makes love with itself.

Thus, we know ourselves to be —
Conscious Life.

It's no wonder humankind concocts creation myths and spins spiritual strategies in an attempt to make some sense of it all and bring it under control.

We are in an awesome situation, and one that often feels overwhelming in its enormity and complexity. Yet we are cognizant creatures, aware that we are conscious; and in that awareness lies our most valued guide.

"As a boy studying Buddhism in Tibet," explains His Holiness the 14th Dalai Lama, "I was taught the importance of a caring attitude towards others. Such a practice of non-violence applies to all sentient beings — any living thing that has a mind. No sentient beings want pain, instead all want happiness and we all share these feelings at some basic level. Therefore, because of our interdependence, the more we care for others' well-being, whether we are concerned with human beings, animals or the environment itself, the deeper will be our own fulfillment."

"The supreme insistence of life is that you enter the adventure
of creating yourself."

~ Brian Swimme

4.   THE IMPERFECT PRESENT

"The essence of any religion lies solely in the answer to the question:
What is my relationship to the infinite universe that surrounds me?"

~ Leo Tolstoy

*W*hatever life is we are microcosms of a mysterious totality. We are paradoxically bound within a membrane that allows for our own uniqueness while being inseparable from the whole. The confluence of opposite, yet simultaneous, worlds — that of self with other, mortality with eternity, birth with death, creativity with determinism, certainty with ambiguity, and freedom with bondage — creates in us a yearning for some kind of reconciliation that seems forever out of reach.

"Beauty is mysterious as well as terrible," Dostoevsky
once said. "God and devil are fighting there,
and the battlefield is the heart of man."

It is our *instinct for freedom* — the natural urge of the heart to liberate itself from all limitations, real or imagined — that compels us to engage life as a journey of awakening — a liberating dance with the imperfect present. That strange, contextual tapestry of life with everything, everywhere, called *this moment now* — a place pregnant with totality, endlessly conceiving and dying with both the basic and metaphysical forces of the universe. It is a sacred space, as terrifying and maddening as it is awe-inspiring and miraculous.

Ironically, it's all we have: life.

"A human being is a synthesis of the infinite and the finite, of the temporal and the eternal, of freedom and necessity."

~ **Kierkegaard**

"Most important for grasping the nature of the present moment," explains philosopher Marilyn Nissim-Sabat, "is understanding that present moments have a temporal structure...they bear within them the immediate past and the foreshadowed future. In that sense there is no *standing now*. The 'now' moment, is a process with retentive (immediate past) and protentive (anticipated future) horizons. The present moment is infused with and structured by these flowing temporal horizons, as well as with their experiential content [qualia]. This flowing process is what Edmund Husserl, the founder of phenomenology, referred to as 'lived experience.'"

And if we so choose to consciously enter this 'lived experience' with radical honesty we can awaken here, evoking courage and insight from confusion and chaos, allowing love and compassion to emerge from the mysterious web of life.

"There are beautiful and wild forces within us," said St Francis of Assisi.

Let us find our own. Learn to love them, trust them.

Acting from our own beautiful wildness, be guided by these liberating forces and compose new-life rhythms, manifesting your finest visions and dreams.

"From the living fountain of instinct flows everything that is creative," Carl Jung once said. "Hence the unconscious is not merely conditioned by history, but is the very source of the creative impulse. It is like nature herself — prodigiously conservative, and yet transcending her own historical conditions in her acts of creation."

"The ideas that have lighted my way have been kindness, beauty, and truth."

~ Albert Einstein

What are the ideas illuminating your way of living?
What are the beautiful wild forces within you?

5. DHARMA INTELLIGENCE

"He lives the poetry that he cannot write. The others write
the poetry that they dare not realize."

~ Oscar Wilde

*E*xpress your life as vividly as you can and give yourself over to the person that you most want to be.

The *dharma*, our own unique dance with existence, serves to transform the suffering within the imperfect present, and evolves our ability to liberate our dreams.

There is nowhere better to enact the metamorphosis but here.

I see no higher *dharma* outside of this.

"*Dharma* — is an ancient Sanskrit word meaning: the inmost constitution of a thing, the law of its inner being, which hastens its growth and without which it ceases to exist," states Nikhilananda, the Indian author and philosopher. "In order to be true to oneself one must act according to one's *dharma*. To mold one's actions according to the law of one's own being is therefore the *dharma*, the way to liberation, of every individual."

It is up to each of us to find our own unique way — our own *Dharma* — and to be as courageous and experimental in its expression as we can.

The most daring realization is to live as an authentic human being, bringing our most intelligent, uncensored aliveness into all aspects of our life.

"Follow your inner moonlight; don't hide the madness."

~ Allen Ginsberg

Pema Chödrön, the American Buddhist nun, elaborates the *Dharma* this way: "The fixed idea that we have about ourselves [can be] painfully limiting. ...To train to stay open and curious...in dissolving the barriers that we erect between ourselves and the world — is [to] train in awakening...[the] nurturing [of] the fundamental flexibility of our being...It manifests as inquisitiveness, as adaptability, as humor, as playfulness.

"It is [also] our capacity to relax with not knowing, not figuring everything out, with not being at all sure about who we are — or who anyone else is either."

The whisper of dharma intelligence is always there, in everything we do.

Can we hear it?

6.   BETRAY THE AGE

"*We* have reached a point at which we must either consciously desire and choose and determine the future of the Earth or submit to such an involvement in our destructiveness that the Earth, and ourselves with it, must certainly be destroyed," writer-poet Wendell Berry warns.

We are the matter of the universe — a Cosmos that made us and will take us. We are genetically encoded to seek and create life, genetically encoded to disintegrate and die. Although we appear to be different, we're all kin beneath the skin, sharing the same ancient ancestry.

From a molecule of DNA — origin unknown — life emerged on Earth. Over the next four and a half billion years we crawled out of the oceans, formed hands and lungs, and walked upright for the first time a mere three hundred thousand years ago. Only one hundred thousand years ago the planet's population was 60,000.

Anthropologists tell us that about 10,000 or so people from the original tribe migrated north from central Africa and from there, spread throughout the world.

And not surprisingly, wherever modern Homo sapiens migrated he and she drove the indigenous peoples into extinction, either by out-producing them or exterminating them through murderous acts of conquest.

"No cause is left but the most ancient of all, the one, in fact, that from the beginning of our history, has determined the very existence of politics, the cause of freedom versus tyranny."

~ Hannah Arendt

Move forward 2,000 years past countless wars, and the rising and passing of civilizations, into a 20th century fraught with obscene brutality: Stalin; Mao; The Holocaust; Hiroshima; genocide in Armenia, Rwanda, Bosnia, and Sudan; Pinochet's terror in Chile; Pol Pot's Cambodia; Apartheid; The crushing of human rights in Syria, Burma, the Congo, and Tibet.

All in the name of what?
Freedom? Democracy? Christ? Capitalism? Allah? Oil? God?

"It is no measure of mental health to be well adjusted to a profoundly sick society."

~ Krishnamurti

Bono, the singer for the rock group U2, gives us his take on the story and moreover, how to turn it around: "There's a truly great Irish poet, Brendan Kennelly," he tells us. "And he has this epic poem called *The Book of Judas*, and there's a line in it that says: 'If you want to serve the age, betray it.'

What does that mean, to betray the age?

"Well to me betraying the Age means exposing its conceits, its foibles, its phony moral certitudes. It means telling the secrets of the age and facing harsher truths."

"In this possibly terminal phase of human existence, democracy and freedom are more than just ideals to be valued — they may be essential to survival."

~ Noam Chomsky

What are the ideas worth betraying?
What are the secrets you wish to tell?
And when will you tell them?

"One of the greatest gifts we can give to another generation is our experience, our wisdom."

~ Desmond Tutu

7. COMPASSIONATE AWARENESS

"Most of the things we do, we do for no better reason than that our fathers have done them or that our neighbors do them, and the same is true of a larger part than we suspect of what we think."

~ Oliver Wendell Holmes

W*e* are in the opening years of a new millennium. Thousands of generations have brought us to the era of the post-modern human — a complex circuitry of (techno-) biological contingency that in order to survive urgently needs to learn how to more intelligently inhabit a compassionate awareness. Because, at the moment, our species is on a trajectory of deep misguidedness and social injustice that might well have a terminal end: thousands of people are dying every day in Africa, needlessly, from the pandemic of AIDS; all major ecosystems are degrading as a result of long-term aggressive exploitation; species are becoming extinct; our pollutants are turning the atmosphere into toxic gas; the oceans are projected to lose all commercial fish stocks by 2048 and many millions of dollars will be spent today (everyday) on war, on maiming, on killing.

"Nothing determines who we will become so much as those things we choose to ignore."

~ Sandor Minab

"When speaking in various countries, one of the questions I am frequently asked," explains Lester Brown, President of Earth Policy Institute, "is given the environmental problems that the world is facing, can we make it? That is, can we avoid the collapse of civilization? My answer is always the same: It depends on you and me. It means becoming politically active. Saving our civilization is not a spectator sport."

"The time is always right to do what is right."

~ Martin Luther King, Jr.

8.   HOLY CURIOSITY

"Human life is a journey whose end is not in sight. Searching, longing and questioning is in our DNA. Who we are and what we will become is determined by the questions that animate us, and by those we refuse to ask. Your questions are your quest. As you ask, so shall you be."

~ Sam Keen

We must remain open and inquisitive, but ultimately, acknowledge the essential mystery of it all. Clearly, we are only in the earliest stages of answering the big questions: knowing what life is, and how it all started. Are we alone in the universe? What's on the other side of death? Is immortality possible? How much of what we perceive is brain-generated projection and how much of it actually exists separate from our minds?

What is the "really real," the "wholly other"?

It was Socrates who, when asked for his definition of wisdom, gave as his conclusion: "knowing that you don't know."

"Favor the question, always question," stated Holocaust survivor and Nobel Peace laureate Elie Wiesel, in reminding us of the gift we can give each other. "Do not accept answers as definitive. Answers change. Questions don't. Always question those who are certain of what they are saying. Always favor the person who is tolerant enough to understand that there are no absolute answers, but there are absolute questions."

In other words: don't stop asking.

We have just begun to probe the galaxies. We are mere infants in a universe governed by a cosmological clock tuned to infinity. Our scientific discoveries are constantly improving descriptions. But these are descriptions, not explanations.

The pre-eminent physicist Michio Kaku tells us, "We have come a long way intellectually from the time of Giordano Bruno, burned at the stake in 1600 by the church for saying that the sun was nothing but a star. But as a species we are in our infancy and just beginning to break free from the imprisonment of gravity."

"The wisdom of inquiry is that the more we question the nature of the world the larger and more compelling our world becomes," states Buddhist scholar Martin Kovan. "It grows beyond us in its mystery, and encompasses those concerns of the self that so readily absorb us," he continues. "On the other hand, the shadow of questioning is that it can work in reverse order: the wonder of the macrocosm can be reduced to the needs of convenient truths found only in what satisfies the hunger of 'I, me, mine — the ego.'"

Aleksandr Solzhenitsyn says it this way: "It is not because the truth is too difficult to see that we make mistakes. We make mistakes because the easiest and most comfortable course for us is to seek insight where it accords with our emotions — especially selfish ones."

Hence Einstein turned towards the
always expansive question in which we,
"Never lose a holy curiosity,"
whether human, global, or divine.

9.   AN OPEN SPACE

*W*e are in a circumstance where anything can happen, and does. Every second is a mysterious twist of infinite cosmic fate and our individual lives reflect only a microscopic unit of it. If I am not hiding in delusion, then I am standing in the naked nirvana of reverential uncertainty, occupying as many dimensions of being as my heart can bear and has the wisdom to embrace.

If I can stand here, I am standing in a pure awareness of life, without the distorting filters that distance me from that which I am: an OPEN SPACE — large and small, weak and strong, transparent and veiled, vulnerable and powerful, unprotected, naked, mortal, and utterly mysterious.

"Nobody can teach me who I Am."

~ **Chinua Achebe**

Within this space, have only the faith in
trusting your deepest life experience.

Listen to the voice within. Listen to your heart.
Don't be afraid of the universe.

"Deserve your dream."

~ **Octavio Paz**

10.   TO GO BEYOND

"The visible universe is but a storehouse of images and signs to which
the imagination will give a relative place and value; it is a pasture
which the imagination must digest and transform."

~ **Charles Baudelaire**

*C*an we ignite an awe of existence — a wonderment that
includes the complexities of our daily life, tender and fragile
as we are? Is it possible, at this time, with all we know, to be
that stirred by the everyday conditions of being? And where
exactly is the intelligence that compels us to rethink our
priorities, our attitudes — the entire way we view the world,
ourselves and our relationships?

"Time after time I have worked with actors," explains Peter
Brook, the innovative British theater and film director, "who
are tragically incapable, however hard they try, of laying
down for one brief instant, even in rehearsal, the image of
themselves that has hardened around an inner emptiness."

"The illiterate of the future are not those who cannot read or
write," states Alvin Toffler. "They are those who cannot learn,
unlearn, and relearn."

How do we learn to live in this entirely new way?

Is it something we can learn?

"The day came when the risk it took to remain tight in a bud
became more painful than the risk it took to blossom."

~ **Anais Nin**

Harley Swift Deer, a Native American teacher, explains that "each of us has a survival dance and a sacred dance... Our survival dance...is what we do for a living — our way of supporting ourselves physically and economically...Once you have your survival dance established, you can wander, inwardly and outwardly, searching for clues to your sacred dance, the work you were born to do."

"Dream dreams and see visions welling up from the preconscious," Rollo May encourages us, as a means to liberate our unrealized potentials. Allow for the "outreaching of the conscious mind to be flooded with ideas, impulses, images and every sort of psychic phenomena," he concludes.

Are you outreaching?

Aristotle defined *entelechy* as "the condition in which a potentiality has become an actuality."

In other words, empower the most vital forces within you that motivate and guide you toward fullness and freedom.

"Let the beauty of what you love be what you do."

~ **Rumi**

11.   ACTIVELY ENGAGED

"Emancipation from the bondage of the soil is no freedom for the tree."

~ **Rabindranath Tagore**

Dharma intelligence is actualized to the extent that we genuinely feel ourselves as contextual beings. In other words, as the biosphere is the intricate web of life on the Earth's surface, our every second of existence is interwoven into that web, into those very same forces that sustain life — all life.

"When we look deep into the heart of a flower, we see clouds, sunshine, minerals, time, the earth, and everything else in the cosmos in it," writes the Vietnamese Buddhist monk, Thich Nhat Hanh. "Without clouds there could be no rain, and there would be no flower." The renowned Indian philosopher J. Krishnamurti speaks to the seamless unity of consciousness saying, "There is no division, psychologically, between us all. We are the world and the world is us. That is not an intellectual theory, but an actuality, to be felt, realized and lived."

We are simultaneously unique and yet indistinguishable from the whole. We are everywhere at once and at the same time challenged to come to terms with our apparent separateness and mortality. As the awareness of non-separation transforms from thought to feeling there is a shift from identification with 'my' circle of friends, 'my' community, 'my' nation and so on — into a clear realization of our innate interrelatedness wherever we are, even when alone. Essentially, one feels more involved with the whole of life — environmentally, psychologically, spiritually, and politically — knowing that one's thoughts and actions have consequences that affect the quality of life for everyone and everything, everywhere.

"I knew someone had to take the first step
and I made up my mind not to move."

~ Rosa Parks

By a simple act of civil disobedience Rosa Parks planted the seed of equality, the freedom of all peoples to live equally everywhere. She created a cultural equation which still carries force for us today — a *meme* for the ages.

"A meme is a pattern of information, held in memory, which is capable of being replicated — transmitted to another individual's memory," states Kalle Lasn. "A meme can be a theory, a phrase, a tune, a concept, a religion, a notion of fashion, philosophy or politics," he goes on to say. "Memes pass through a population in much the same way genes pass through a species. Potent memes can change minds, alter behavior, catalyze collective shifts in consciousness and transform cultures. In our information age, whoever makes the memes holds the power," he concludes.

Adbusters, "a global network of culture jammers and creatives working to change the way information flows, the way corporations wield power, and the way meaning is generated in our society," produced a poster for their annual *Buy Nothing Day* stating: "Suddenly, we ran out of money and, to avoid collapse, we quickly pumped liquidity back into the system. But behind our financial crisis a much more ominous crisis looms: We are running out of nature: fish, forests, fresh water, minerals, soil. What are we going to do when supplies of these vital resources run low? There's only one way to avoid the collapse of this human experiment of ours on Planet Earth: we have to consume less. It will take a massive mind shift. You can start...by buying nothing on November 28th. Then...make a resolution to change your lifestyle...It's now or never!"

"Every individual has a responsibility to help guide our global family in the right direction. Good wishes are not sufficient; we must become *actively engaged.*"

~ 14th Dalai Lama

12. RAW AND NERVY

*A*s we learn to more consciously evolve our *dharma intelligence* — the liberating wisdom inherent in consciousness — greater dimensions of reality are illuminated. As falsity is revealed, we realign towards truth.

Being guided by our voice of freedom and dignity often defies logic and reasoning. As our passion for liberation increases we take greater risks, become more daring. This usually means challenging compromise and fear and entering the jaws of raw, tumultuous existence. It's worth remembering that finding our liberation through living often agitates the suppressed apathy or anger driving self-centered striving. But as Nietzsche declared, "You need chaos in your soul to give rise to a dancing star."

E. L. Doctorow says it this way: "We're always attracted to the edges of what we are. Out on the edge where it's a little raw and nervy." And it is a bit nervy to peel off false faces and live from our uncensored wildness.

> "The opposite of courage is not cowardice, it is conformity."
>
> ~ Rollo May

Some social forces seek to control us by manipulating the conditions for whatever shame can be found. And shame requires buying into a value system that doesn't belong to anyone in particular; more often an illusion assumed as a given truth — such as the one Rosa Parks exposed for its falsehood. So when you release your shame you discover a radical new source of power and beauty.

So live it. Feel it.
Become alive to it.
Embody your raw nervy truth and set yourself free.
Reawaken total being.
Blaze your own trail.

Turn your life into an epic adventure, even if it means defying social mores or breaking taboos that attempt to suppress and control your impulses. It's my sense that when compromise or doubt no longer holds appeal, you will see the "dancing star" on the horizon of your mystery. And when you do, move with it, dance with it, follow your joy, until there's no turning back from the guiding light of what you really love, and leave the rest behind.

"I am often asked about life in prison," writes Ahmed Kathrada in his book *Simple Freedom*. "Here is a passage from a letter I wrote (after twenty-five years in [South African] jails) to a young couple on the verge of marriage:

"The stereotyped image of a prison is one of forbidding high walls; a grim, cold atmosphere, prosaic, harsh, vulgar, violent; an atmosphere of desperate, unsmiling faces; angry, bitter, and frustrated beings. Admittedly, a prison situation is tailor-made for the projection of such an image...It is easy to succumb when faced with prospects of a lengthy and nightmarish existence and consequently dwell on one's miseries, hardships, the manifold deprivations and negative experiences.

"Someone has written about two prisoners looking out of their cell window — the one saw iron bars while the other saw stars. How true!"

"There is no passion to be found by playing small — in settling for a life that is less than the one you are capable of living,"

Nelson Mandela tells us.

"It always seems impossible until it's done."

13.   USE YOUR FREEDOM

"I saw the Angel in the stone and carved it to set it free."

~ **Michelangelo**

Coming to terms with our deepest sense of purpose requires a dedication to fulfilling a dream. Inevitably, this takes us from ordinary comforts and private concerns and thrusts us down a wild existential highway few dare to travel. Not only will taking up the art and activism of freedom break our contracts with conditionality, exposing how we grasp and brace and hold back, it will confront the entire apparatus of avoidance — every fear, every complicity, and every nuance of self-deception.

Breaking free from fear-driven presence, we re-inspire our courage again and again, until we truly understand that our dignity is our greatest worth and that our *dharma intelligence* is the instinctual wisdom that will most effectively guide us in transforming this maddening miracle of life.

"Integrity simply means a willingness not to violate one's identity."

~ **Erich Fromm**

The visionary filmmaker and professor, Trinh T. Minh-ha, tells us that "Students often find it very difficult to assume freedom; when you give them freedom they experience it as chaos. It is very hard for many of them to accept that we can be confused together and because of that strain of being confused together, we can move somewhere else, with and beyond the place in which we have been confined. The difficulty lies in accepting this moment of so-called confusion, the moment of blankness and of emptiness through which one necessarily passes in order to have insight."

One place where confusion becomes valuable, blankness naturally spacious and emptiness ultimately fertile, is in the creative realm.

"Both artists and neurotics speak and live from the subconscious and unconscious depths of their society," Rollo May writes. "The artist does this positively, communicating what he and she experiences to his and her fellow men and women. The neurotic does this negatively."

> Be an artist of your experience, its accomplice in
> the transgression of self-censorship. It's only the
> neurotic in us who fears we might be getting it

> wrong.

"It's life that matters, nothing but life — the process of discovering, the everlasting and perpetual process, not the discovery itself, at all."

~ **Fyodor Dostoyevsky**

14.   LIFE, OUR ART

"The creative process is a cocktail of instinct, skill, culture and a highly creative feverishness," Francis Bacon writes. "It is a particular state when everything happens very quickly, a mixture of consciousness and unconsciousness, of fear and pleasure; it's a little like making love..."

*D*harma intelligence should not be confused with transcendence — an attempt to escape oneself or the world. The artistry of embodied freedom has nothing to do with life-denying attitudes that suppress oneself into status quo submission. Nor am I proposing some idea of 'primordial beingness' as the only true means to address the complexities of life or to subdue human suffering. Radical freedom requires an awareness that is life-giving, not fear-driven. It includes the flesh and spirit, paradox and ambiguity, materiality and immanence — the sacred and mundane as one.

It's about making life our art.

Georgia O'Keeffe explains it this way: "One day seven years ago I found myself saying to myself — I can't live where I want to — I can't go where I want to go — I can't do what I want to — I can't even say what I want to — so I decided I was a very stupid fool not to at least paint as I wanted to."

"Be your own person and resist following others' ideals," Deng Ming-Dao writes in *The Chronicles of Tao*. "Filling yourself with the thinking of other people limits you. Realize your own nature by yourself. Be free to be yourself. Know yourself; bring what is within you to fruition."

Choosing freedom as a creative process is essentially a multitude of liberating actions manifested over a lifetime; actions that include savoring our tiny joys and insights all along the way.

Pablo Casals, the Spanish cellist who died at the age of 96, once said, "My work is my life. I cannot think of one without the other. To 'retire' means to me to begin to die. The man who works and is never bored is never old. Each day I am reborn. For the past eighty years I have started each day in the same manner. It is not a mechanical routine but something essential to my daily life. I go to the piano and I play two preludes and fugues of Bach. It is a sort of benediction on the house. It fills me with awareness of the wonder of life, with a feeling of the incredible marvel of human being. The music is never the same to me. Each day it is something new, fantastic and unbelievable, like nature, a miracle."

"There is a sixth sense, the religious sense, the sense of wonder."

~ D.H. Lawrence

15. BEFRIEND YOURSELVES

"I define self as the interiorization of community."

~ **James Hillman**

Include every moment, every encounter, every aspect of your nature — as sacred to the whole.

"All growth is a leap in the dark, a spontaneous unpremeditated act without the benefit of experience," Henry Miller once said.

Be bold.

Leap!

And from such an inclusive embrace of life, explore freedom's true function — to be free, right now.

Imagine being a pianist, a painter or a parent and losing your hands. Imagine then getting them back, and the gratitude you would feel for the freedom that your hands and fingers provide you. The idea is to have our hands and hearts on life as much as we can — aware that we can lose that privilege at any time — playing and shaping the rhythms and forms that most touch us.

"Do I contradict myself? Very well, then I contradict myself, I am large, I contain multitudes."

~ **Walt Whitman**

And by occupying freedom it grows.

Or as Bob Dylan so famously said,
"He who is not busy being born is busy dying."

In other words, every second is a creative choice to
exercise our freedom, express it — be it!

"If you do not express your own original ideas, if you do not listen to
your own being, then you will have betrayed yourself."

~ Rollo May

Philip Roth, the American novelist, in speaking about the inherent trust in his creative process, writes: "All I can tell you with certainty is that I, for one, have no self, and that I am unwilling or unable to perpetrate upon myself the joke of a self ... What I have instead is a variety of impersonations I can do, and not only of myself — a troupe of players that I have internalised, a permanent company of actors that I can call upon when a self is required....I am a theater and nothing more than a theater."

Sometimes I stop and ask myself how deeply do I trust my own authenticity.

How dependent am I on other people's mental life?

What does bravery mean to me?

"Inner freedom comes from following a course in harmony
with one's conscience."

~ Aung San Suu Kyi

16.   TRUE SANITY

"All men and women should strive to learn before they die what they are running from, and to, and why."

~ James Thurber

*O*nce we start to accept the magnificent, weird beauty of being human — alive as hyper-conscious, biologically constituted creatures — honoring our uniqueness, our contradictions, our strengths and foibles too — we begin to live more engaged, creative lives. We are less beholden to images of how we think we should look. We hold ourselves with greater dignity. We listen to the voices of instinct and intuition more fully. We use our imagination more. We dream more freely. We take greater risks. We are no longer afraid of being who we are; manifesting our most courageous-outrageous sense of self.

"Most people are other people," Oscar Wilde once quipped. "Their thoughts are someone else's opinions, their lives a mimicry, their passions a quotation."

As our authenticity matures even our most cherished identities seem to vanish — being punk, pink, a philanthropist, or eco-cool; or an evolutionary Buddhist, or a spiritual revolutionary, or an edgy performer, a radical activist, an author, a rock star yoga teacher, or even a seeker — leaving just this sense of our most natural human beingness, relating intimately, consciously, courageously with the flow of life in this moment now, the imperfect present. At different times, poetic, ordinary, dazzling, wild, erotic, brilliant, terrified, surreal. Truthfulness guides authenticity — the tireless integrity to be courageously real and transparent, integrating both the creative and diabolical forces of the universe — transforming them for the enrichment of one's own being and the betterment of all life.

"To be nobody but yourself in a world which is doing its best, night and day, to make you everybody else," writes e. e. cummings, "means to fight the hardest battle which any human being can fight, and never stop fighting."

Socrates mirrored the doomed shallowness of the State by challenging its policy of "might is right" with his notion of "goodness and justice."

Before being forced to drink the hemlock that killed him, he declared: "Better that the mass of mankind should disagree... and contradict me than I be out of harmony with myself."

R.D. Laing writes, "True sanity entails...the dissolution of the normal ego, that false self competently adjusted to our alienated social reality... [and from] this death a rebirth, and the eventual re-establishment of a new servant of the divine, no longer its betrayer."

"No price is too high to pay for the privilege of owning yourself."
~ Friedrich Nietzsche

How do you let other people's perceptions define you?

What are the next steps in becoming a revitalized servant of your own unique genius?

17.   NO TURNING BACK

"Too much sanity may be madness and the maddest of all, to see life as it is and not as it should be."

~ Miguel de Cervantes

*W*e exist on earth for a brief time.

Life is an experience that is always interrupted.

What would it feel like to be in the final days of our life?

It's certainly happening, whether we think it or not.

The point is, to live every moment as if it counts.

Because it does.

It's all we have.

Bono, of U2, spoke of his first meeting with the late US Congressman Thomas Lantos, saying: "I met this incredible man...a survivor of the concentration camps and he told me that years later it wasn't the brutality in the camps that haunted him, but the blank stares of the faces as they were loaded onto the trains. And this is a very heavy thing to bring up but there is some analogy here. He said, "Oh no, it's worse than that, because we knew where those trains were going."

[Now, in Africa and in other places all over the world] Bono continued, "We are letting children die for lack of medicines you can get in any corner shop. And so I asked him if I could use the analogy and he said "Yes." And that's what our generation has to do.

"We've got to go down and lie across the tracks."

In describing his liberation into activism Vaclav Havel said that "I had stopped waiting for the world to improve and exercised my right to intervene in that world." Petra Kelly, co-founder of the German Green Party, stated the need for collective action much more bluntly, saying, "If we, the generation that faces the next century, don't do the impossible; we shall be faced with the unthinkable."

How to do the impossible?

Who really knows, right?

So we start small. Take care of something that's precious to us.

Nurture it. Let it grow. Feel its beauty, our own decency.

And let us consider the prophetic words of Franz Kafka, when he said: "From a certain point onward, there is *no turning back*. That is the point that must be reached."

What will it take for us to reach it?

Tibet's renowned poet-saint, Milarepa,
stated his life's mission this way:

"My religion is to live — and die — without regret."

What actions might you take to "lie across the tracks" in support of your most compelling cause? What actions might you take to "live and die without regret?"

And when might you take them?

> "Ordinarily, a person leaving a courtroom with a conviction behind him would wear a somber face. But I left with a smile. I knew that I was a convicted criminal, but I was proud of my crime."
>
> ~**Martin Luther King, Jr., March 22, 1956**

18.   INTEGRITY

"Sanity is a madness put to good use."

~ **George Santayana**

*W*e become human by occupying greater dimensions of our entire selves; our bodies, our breath, our hearts, our hurts, our joys, our creativity, our imagination, and our intelligence— as much of ourselves as we have the courage to enter and embrace. We must not be so afraid of life that we choose the comfort of illusions or find asylum in fear, repression or denial.

Let us summon the heart and wisdom to engage the nuances of our being. Why marginalize anything, inside or outside? Sure, there are some pretty ugly things in this world. But why allow this certainty to discredit magic or mystery? Why not insist on going forward with conviction and conscience. Why not be forthright and innovative in our expressions of caring, in our activism, in our art, in everything we do, and so transform this vastness into something less maddening and more magical, whatever that may be.

"We can re-invent civil disobedience in a million different ways," writes Arundhati Roy. "In other words, we can come up with a million different ways of becoming a collective pain in the ass. Our strategy should be not only to confront empire but to lay siege to it. To deprive it of oxygen. To shame it. To mock it. With our art, our music, our brilliance, our sheer relentlessness — and our ability to tell our own stories. Stories different than the ones we are brainwashed to believe."

She goes on to say, "The corporate revolution will collapse if we refuse to buy what it is selling — their ideas, their version of history, their wares, their weapons, their notion of inevitability. Remember this: We are many and they few. They need us more than we need them."

> "The first principal of nonviolent action is that of
> non-cooperation with everything humiliating."
>
> ~ Cesar Chavez

"I just got home from talking to a new friend, another longtime activist," writes Derrick Jensen. "She told me of a campaign she participated in a few years ago to try to stop the government and transnational timber corporations from spraying Agent Orange, a potent defoliant and teratogen, in the forests of Oregon. Whenever activists learned a hillside was going to be sprayed, they assembled there, hoping their presence would stop the poisoning. But each time, like clockwork, helicopters appeared, and each time, like clockwork, helicopters dumped loads of Agent Orange onto the hillside and onto protesting activists. The campaign did not succeed. "But," she said to me, "I'll tell you what did. A bunch of Vietnam vets lived in those hills, and they sent messages to the Bureau of Land Management and to Weyerhaeuser, Boise Cascade, and the other timber companies saying, 'We know the names of your helicopter pilots, and we know their addresses.'" I waited for her to finish. "You know what happened next?" she asked. "I think I do," I responded. "Exactly," she said. "The spraying stopped.""

"We should never forget that everything Adolf Hitler did in Germany was "legal" and everything the Hungarian freedom fighters did in Hungary was "illegal."

~ Martin Luther King, Jr., "Letter from Birmingham Jail," 1963

"In the Nazi concentration camps the basic message of fairy stories stayed with me," psychologist Bruno Bettleheim explains. "That in life you encounter terrible events, but if you can hold onto your values, you might survive and be better for it."

"One of the truest tests of *integrity* is its blunt refusal to be compromised."

~ Chinua Achebe

19. LIBERATING FREEDOM

> "And I think that you too would call it propaganda when people are
> enticed into a change of opinion by promises of pleasure, or terrified into
> it by threats. Yes, propaganda and deceit always go together."
>
> ~ **Plato, *The Republic***

*L*iberating the mind from orthodoxies requires extracting freedom from its inherited delusions, political manipulations, and suffocating mythologies. We must come to understand that freedom is essential to our survival. It might be manipulated by ideology, propaganda, and prejudice but let us remain vigilant in separating freedom from the packaging and additives our political-spiritual consumer culture has manufactured around it.

Howard Zinn, the late American human rights advocate and author, wrote, "If those in charge of our society — politicians, corporate executives, and owners of press and television — can dominate our ideas, they will be secure in their power. They will not need soldiers patrolling the streets. We will control ourselves."

To safeguard ourselves against unconscious self-servitude, remember: Freedom has no logo, no identity, and no nationality.

Like the wind, it doesn't belong to anyone.
Nor can it be grasped or held.

> "I wish that every human life might be pure transparent freedom."
>
> ~ **Simone de Beauvoir**

As you liberate your understanding of freedom,
freedom itself liberates all that still resists it.

"All one can do is to achieve nakedness, to be what one is with all one's
faculties and perceptions, strengthened by all the skill which one can acquire,
and then to stand before the judgment of time."

~ Stephen Spender

20.   AUTHENTICITY

Elevating authenticity to its highest status requires a radical acceptance of who you are and feel yourself to be — inhabiting every dimension of your being as natural to your entirety. What else do we have but our humanness, our naturalness, our own unique selves?

"I've been imitated so well I've heard people copy my mistakes."

~ Jimi Hendrix

No two of us are alike. No two of us have the same fingerprint. No two minds are the same, no matter how much we have in common.

No two people love in the same way.
Imagine a 'law' on the "right way" to kiss?
It's Orwellian, isn't it?

Or the 'intimately correct' way to smile?
Or the religiously correct way to know God as
a Christian or Nirvana as a Buddhist.

Or knowing the 'Absolute True Enlightenment' of any so-called Saint as one's 'own enlightenment,' and then 'bestowing' or 'disavowing' that Certainty onto others?

Conformity is a bit like that, isn't it? Lock-step is antithetical to uniqueness. So too with the way each of us make love. Intimacy embodies our most natural freedom, our most authentic sensitivities. That's why it's sacred.

Imagine imposing a commandment on the spiritually correct expression of the erotic? Or the existentially correct way to despair, or cry, or create, or be free?

When in doubt I remind myself: I am the freedom that I seek. Live outward from there.

"I freed thousands of slaves, Harriet Tubman declared.
"And I could have freed thousands more, if
they had only known they were slaves."

21. REWILD YOUR PSYCHE

"Every human being is a reflection of the universe," writes Danish artist and composer Christian Skeel. "How can we be different from our origins? We are all a product of the Source. [And] between the Source and ourselves we place mirrors and paintings, text and dance, music and theories, prayers and sport, meditation and experiments, in order to be, to feel, to learn. This is art. This is science."

*A*s fragrance is innate to a flower, so too is freedom inherent to the heart. This is as obvious as standing out in the wild and asking, "Where is nature found?" It's all around us, and in us. When we know nature as such, we wake up, begin living again, and in some ways we stop dying inside; stop succumbing to thoughts and feelings and images that undermine our spontaneity, our daring, our creativity, our own unique subjective sense of self — strange and beautiful as we are.

Transforming our lives into a liberating journey of awakening is not about conforming to some ready made solution or transcending some imaginary problem — often constructed by religion — to make you feel bad about yourself until you have the 'faith' to feel good again.

Let us also be vigilant in cutting through ideologies that valorize fear and greed, whether in our living rooms, school rooms, or halls of 'higher education,' where young minds are often shaped into consumers, characterized by conformity, competition, and a denial of one's impact on nature, on the future of life itself.

> Huck Finn to Tom Sawyer, in complaining about conformity at the home of straight-laced Widow Douglas, said: "'I've tried it, and it don't work; it don't work, Tom. It ain't for me ... The widder eats by a bell; she goes to bed by a bell; she gets up by a bell —everything's so awful reg'lar a body can't stand it.'"
> ~ **Mark Twain**, *The Adventures of Tom Sawyer*

Rewild your psyche, open your mind and pour forth a new form, one that cannot be reproduced or restrained. There is no copyright on freedom nor on the 'true voice' of nature. Let your quest transform old worlds and create new ones: unpremeditated, unknown.

> "It's surprising how many persons go through life without ever recognizing that their feelings toward other people are largely determined by their feelings toward themselves."
> ~ **Sydney J. Harris**

Sapphire, the American author and performance poet, states: "Self-hatred keeps a lot of people's energy and creativity sapped. The very forces that could be harnessed to fight fascism and imperialism are being drained off into 'fitting in' and 'being accepted.'"

"This, I believe, is the great truth," Joseph Campbell writes. "That each of us is a completely unique creature and that, if we are ever to give any gift to the world, it will have to come out of our own experience and fulfillment of our own potentialities, not someone else's."

To inhabit our most liberating expression of being requires challenging fear and doing something remarkable with our lives.

"I'm not telling you to make the world better, explains Joan Didion, "I'm just telling you to live in it. Not just to endure it, not just to suffer it, not just to pass through it, but to live in it. To look at it. To try to get the picture. To do your own work. To take chances. To live recklessly. To seize the moment. And if you ask me why you should bother to do that, I could tell you that the grave's a fine and private place, but none I think do there embrace. Nor do they sing there, or write, or argue, or see the tidal bore on the Amazon, or touch their children.

"And that's what there is to do and *get it while you can...*"

22. THE ETIQUETTE OF FREEDOM

*O*n the one hand, we see ourselves as a separate being seeking to develop our own individual life, while on the other we are trying to understand and participate in a much greater whole. The *dharma life* — our own unique way of finding liberation through living — is both an inner and an outer dance.

> At times more focus falls on one than the other.
> At other times they flow in seamless mutuality.

How each of us goes about transforming existence and embodying new dimensions of being — is personal. While there's no singular, true way, there is one innate calling that leads to many expressions of the same answer — *liberation*.

That one yearning may best be expressed in the simple words of *The Serenity Prayer* by Reinhold Niebuhr: "God, grant me the serenity to accept the things I cannot change, the courage to change the things I can and the wisdom to *know* the difference."

> To *know* is the operative word — the ability to recognize
> one's own identity and its expression in the world. This,
> according to Abraham Maslow, "...is, in essence, the
> search for one's own intrinsic, authentic values."

Gary Snyder points out, "The world is our consciousness, and it surrounds us. There are more things in mind, in the imagination, than 'you' can keep track of — thoughts, memories, images, angers, delights, rise unbidden. The depths of mind, the unconscious, are our inner wilderness areas."

If you turn to a mentor you look for a guide, not one who is embedded in the predictability of orthodoxy, but one who knows, as Snyder puts it, the "etiquette of freedom" — the liberating authenticity of being true to yourself.

We read in the traditional Buddhist texts of a teaching the Buddha gave to his son Rahula on the "etiquette of freedom." They were walking in the forest when the Buddha stopped and asked Rahula, "What is the function of a mirror?"

"For reflection," Rahula replied.

To which the Buddha responded "Indeed. So too, use your mind like a mirror. Reflect on whatever you think, say, and do. And upon reflection, if you know it may harm you and others, refrain from those expressions. And if you know upon reflection that it may benefit you and others, cultivate it. Thus, by using your mind like a mirror, Rahula, reflect: learn to know yourself in this way, night and day."

"In the Buddhist tradition, people used to speak of 'enlightenment' as a kind of returning home...the recovery of oneself, of one's integrity."

~ Thich Nhat Hanh

23.   LEARN TO DISCERN

There is a famous Burmese Buddhist saying that goes like this: "Those who know, know both those who know and those who don't know. Those who don't know, know neither. The main thing, however, is to know what you know, and how you came to know it, as well as know what you don't know, and how you could know it."

The essence of this statement is: learn to discern the difference between the direct personal experience of something — the facts, the truth, the reality of that thing — and the projections, beliefs, and opinions it inspires.

R. D. Laing said it this way: "The range of what we think and do is limited by what we fail to notice. And because we fail to notice that we fail to notice, there is little we can do to change; until we notice how failing to notice shapes our thoughts and deeds."

As we increasingly fail to notice, Gore Vidal explains, "Societies grow decadent, [and] the language grows decadent, too. Words are used to disguise, not to illuminate, action: you liberate a city by destroying it. Words are to confuse so that at election time people will solemnly vote against their own interests." Thus, the manipulation of the mind occurs, or in the words of Noam Chomsky, we have what is known as "the manufacturing of consent."

For example, "To us Tibetans the phrase "the liberation of Tibet," in its moral and spiritual implications, is based upon a deadly mockery. The country of a free people was invaded and occupied under the pretext of liberation — liberation from whom and what? Ours was a happy country with a solvent Government and a contented people until the Chinese invasion in 1950."

~ "Manifesto by Tibetan Leaders" International Commission of Jurists
— The Question of Tibet and the Rule of Law, 1959

Doublethink is an integral concept in George Orwell's dystopian novel *1984*.

According to the novel "doublethink" is: "The power of holding two contradictory beliefs in one's mind simultaneously, and accepting both of them. To tell deliberate lies while genuinely believing in them, to forget any fact that has become inconvenient, and then, when it becomes necessary again, to draw it back from oblivion for just so long as it is needed, to deny the existence of objective reality and all the while to take account of the reality which one denies — all this is indispensably necessary."

Carl Jung reminds us that "We should know what our convictions are, and stand for them. Upon one's own philosophy, conscious or unconscious, depends one's ultimate interpretation of the facts. Therefore it is wise to be as clear as possible about one's subjective principles. As the man is, so will be his ultimate truth."

"The historic ascent of humanity, taken as a whole, may be summarizedas a succession of victories of consciousness over blind forces — in nature, in society, in man himself."

~ Leon Trotsky

It might be that of those blind forces, those in us, if we see through them, they will prove to be the most nurturing source of our own integrated awakening.

"What does it take to be genuinely creative?" Sam Keen asks. "The willingness to wrestle with chaos, and engage the dark, destructive forces that threaten the psyche?...Therapy does not leave us whole and unscared, but aware of our wounds. At best, as Freud said, "[it] helps people exchange neurotic suffering for real suffering, neurotic anxiety for realistic fears."

It is a fine line, certainly, perhaps the finest there is, in which we have the freedom to recreate our entire existence, if that is what we want. Anything is possible. Why not?

"Between stimulus and response there is a space. In that space is our power to choose our response. In our response lie our growth and our freedom."

~ **Viktor Frankl**

24.   AWESTRUCK VISION

"Open your eyes, look within. Are you satisfied with the life you're living?"

~ **Bob Marley**

*C*onsciously transforming oneself is obviously a complex undertaking. It is often arduous and all-consuming, requiring heroic patience and determination. At other times, the way is silent, nearly imperceptible.

It can also be a magical dance, whereby we smile as we absorb life's delicious blend of beauty and intrigue. Then, without notice, a storm of torment, origin unknown, sweeps over us and brings us to our knees.

The Canadian philosopher Mark Kingwell in addressing the "enduring vulnerability" of the human condition, writes: "Nobody seems to write songs about the pain. I mean, the long-standing burden of love, the ever-present epoxy of gratitude for one's good fortune mixed with this terrible, unwholesome fear of having its source damaged or taken away ... Awake at night, I place my left hand on the delicate fretwork of Gail's rib cage and feel the slow beating of her heart, wishing I could somehow cup it in my hands and keep it safe. How is it that happiness can include, apparently as a necessary condition, so much potential unhappiness? How is it that love, which brings so much strength, should also entail this enduring vulnerability, this dreadful potential for pain?"

Being alive and engaged with whatever life throws our way is an odyssey no one can prepare us for. No amount of spiritual practice or psychological preparation makes direct experience any less daunting.

"Perhaps everything terrible is in its deepest being is something helpless that wants help from us."

~ **Rainer Maria Rilke**

Daniel Dennett, the American philosopher and author, writes: "If you can approach the world's complexities, both its glories and its horrors, with an attitude of humble curiosity, acknowledging that however deeply you have seen, you have only scratched the surface, you will find worlds within worlds, beauties you could not hitherto imagine, and your own mundane preoccupations will shrink to proper size, not all that important in the greater scheme of things. Keeping that *awestruck vision* of the world ready at hand while dealing with the demands of daily living is no easy exercise. But...if you can stay centered and engaged, you will find the hard choices easier, the right words will come to you when you need them and you will be a better person. That, I propose, is the secret to spirituality."

"The goal of our journey, our quest, is to penetrate the mystery of life's events."

~ **African oral tradition**

And what is the secret to your spirituality?
The goal of your own unique quest?

25.   TO STAY HUMAN

"The oneness of human beings is the basic ethical thread
that holds us together."

~ **Muhammad Yunus**

Before spending time as a journalist in some of the war zones of the world, I assumed that I had some reliable relationship to freedom. It took the often-time insanity of living in those areas to reveal just how contextual and myopic my realization of freedom actually was. Take away the continuity of my comfort, my security, my loved ones, and leave me vulnerable to the cruelty of dictatorship, or embracing a crying infant in a refugee camp with dozens of other traumatized children, or comforting a terrified woman who had been gang-raped by enemy soldiers, and I realized that my wisdom was relative indeed.

In addition, I thought that I had a reasonable understanding of courage, until I saw people sacrifice their lives to save others. I thought I had a respectable level of compassion until I had a stranger shield my body with his from the shrapnel of a mortar attack. These experiences and others rattled my confidence. I came away from those years knowing, without a doubt, that transforming the primitive forces of ignorance found in the heart of every human being is the greatest of all challenges.

It is both humbling and exhilarating,
inspiring awe as well as terror.

Bertrand Russell, in addressing the human predicament and what we can do to help, described life as "A long march through the night, surrounded by invisible foes, tortured by weariness and pain, towards a goal that few can hope to reach, and where none may tarry long. One by one, as [we] march, our comrades vanish from our sight, seized by the silent orders of omnipotent Death. Very brief is the time in which we can help them, in which their happiness or misery is decided."

"Be it ours to shed sunshine on their path," he continues. "To lighten their sorrows by the balm of sympathy, to give them the pure joy of a never-tiring affection, to strengthen failing courage, to instill faith in hours of despair.

"Let us not weigh in grudging scales their merits and demerits, but let us think only of their need — of the sorrows, the difficulties, perhaps the blindness's that make the misery of their lives; let us remember that they are *fellow-sufferers* in the same darkness, actors in the same tragedy as ourselves."

"Sometimes the hardest thing to do is just to stay human."

~ **Michael Franti**

26.　TRY AND UNDERSTAND

Human life as we know it is only seven thousand generations old. The emergence of a cognitive self — which isn't
some centralized interior unit, but a network of complex neu-
ral maps — is still in its infancy. It is my sense that we need
to activate this self, this network of systems, and see it, meta-
phorically, as we would a newborn child. Let us nurture this
self into the most creative and conscious self possible, rather
than see it as the source of suffering.

> Ignorance — not knowing who we are, not
> knowing how to love and give back to life — is the
> source of suffering. Not our own personhood.

> Life is an experience to inhabit, not
> a burning house to escape.

Elie Wiesel, who was able to survive a Nazi concentration
camp for five years, while his mother, father and sister were
killed during those years, was asked in an interview for
O Magazine: "What does it take to be normal again, after
having your humanity stripped away?" He replied, "What is
abnormal is that I am normal. That I survived the Holocaust
and went on to love beautiful girls, to talk, to write, to have
toast and tea and live my life — that is what is abnormal."

Arundhati Roy offers this reflection on the heart of being
human: "To love... [and]...to be loved is the foundation of life.
To never forget your own insignificance. To never get used
to the unspeakable violence and the vulgar disparity of life

around you. To seek joy in the saddest places. To pursue beauty to its lair. To never simplify what is complicated or complicate what is simple. To respect strength, never power. Above all, to watch. To *try and understand*. To never look away. And never, never, to forget."

"Life's errors cry for the merciful beauty that can modulate their isolation into a harmony with the whole."

~ Rabindranath Tagore

"Being happy is not the only happiness," Alice Walker reminds us.

27. VISIONARY INQUIRY

"A shadow will appear dark in proportion to the brilliancy of the light surrounding it and conversely it will be less conspicuous where it is seen against a darker background."

~ Leonardo da Vinci

*F*undamentally, the language of liberation is transconceptual. Freedom is not an ontological technology that can be purchased and programmed into the mind. Rather, *the dharma* is life itself, the world of perception — of gradation, dimension, contrasts. Leading a liberating-intelligent life means walking along a nearly invisible edge that on the one hand accepts our imperfect humanness, and on the other strives towards our visions and goals. It means looking into the future knowing that death is always present. With each out-breath there's no certainty of another in-breath.

It's a journey inward and outward, simultaneously.
Each moment contains the forwards and the backwards.

In a universe without an absolute east or west,
up or down, or past or future, there is only
an uncanny natural simultaneity.

"The search for the present is neither the pursuit of an earthly paradise nor that of a timeless eternity: it is the search for a real reality."

~ Octavio Paz

Here we're called to live in the existential fluidity of the 'everywhere-at-once-ness' of the cosmos, where we can bring an increasing awareness to the dance, transforming a bit of the madness in the miracle, each and every day.

"We're inquiring into the deepest nature of our constitutions," Gerald Edelman, a British neuroscientist, states: "How we inherit from each other. How we can change. How our minds think. How our will is related to our thoughts.

How our thoughts are related to our molecules." *Visionary inquiry* requires an abiding trust in both our intuitive wisdom and the sanity of rational thinking. It also requires a devotion to learning the difference between preconceived opinions and prejudice and actuality — the truth and reality of something.

"Not ignorance, but ignorance of ignorance is the death of knowledge," Alfred North Whitehead once said. "The truth may be puzzling," Carl Sagan explains. "It may be counterintuitive. It may contradict deeply held prejudices. It may not be consonant with what we desperately want to be true. But our preferences do not determine what's true."

"We have to live today by what truth we can get today and be ready tomorrow to call it falsehood."

~ William James

28. OUR SACRED RESPONSIBILITY

"The nature of life on Earth and the search for life elsewhere are two sides of the same question: the search for who we are."

~ Carl Sagan

*I*t's easy to appreciate that the biological intelligence orchestrating the hundred billion neurons in our brains right now is inseparable from the quantum intelligence that unifies every wave and particle of the cosmos. It is extremely difficult, however, to embrace that reality as ultimately beautiful.

It is as it is — phenomenal existence.

We are all finite organic systems, unique and conscious of ourselves, while configured within this infinitely mysterious coherence. This vastness is sacred and is also terrifying in its limitlessness. From this perspective, beauty is no longer continuous with a sense of enchantment. In other words, the big picture does not guarantee wonder. This is because this quantum intelligence has also to account for the devastating ugliness of war, genocide, famine, and human stupidity.

"War perverts and destroys you," states Chris Hedges, author of *Empire of Illusion* and *War is a Force that Gives us Meaning*. "It pushes you closer and closer to your own annihilation — spiritual, emotional and, finally, physical," he continues. "It destroys the continuity of life, tearing apart all systems, economic, social, environmental and political, that sustain us as human beings. War is necrophilia. The essence of war is death. War is a state of almost pure sin with its goals of hatred and destruction. It is organized sadism. War fosters alienation and leads inevitably to nihilism. It is a turning away from the sanctity of life."

"How many does it take to metamorphose wickedness into righteousness? One man must not kill. If he does, it is murder...But a state or nation may kill as many as they please, and it is not murder. It is just, necessary, commendable, and right. Only get enough people to agree to it, and the butchery of myriads of human beings is perfectly innocent. But how many does it take?"

~ Adin Ballou, *The Non-Resistant*, 1845

Charles Darwin offers a perspective on our species that reminds us not to demonize the darkness or the ignorance, but to recognize that we are in this together, both as perpetrator as well as redeemer. "Man with all his noble qualities, with sympathy which feels for the most debased, with benevolence which extends not only to other men but to the humblest living creatures, with his god-like intellect which has penetrated into the movements and constitution of the solar system — with all these exalted powers — man still bears in his bodily frame the indelible stamp of his lowly origin."

Carl Jung once said, "In studying the history of the human mind one is impressed again and again by the fact that the growth of the mind is the widening of the range of consciousness, and that each step forward has been a most painful and laborious achievement."

Clearly, if we are to sustain life on our planet and progress as a species we must discover the deepest structures governing this terrifying and beautiful existence, which is so strangely flawed, and so gorgeous too. This requires a daring exploration of "who we are," integrating our collective insights, in order to evolve the most intelligent relationship with as many dimensions of reality as possible, both internal to and beyond us, as we peacefully explore the Cosmos.

"We have to do the best we can. This is our sacred human responsibility."

~ **Albert Einstein**

29. LIMITLESS MUTUALITY

We cannot live without each other.

This means feeling more than just one's own self-interest, or the interests of one's family. Defining ourselves as nations, sects, and tribes with fixed or rigid ideological borders, is in large part why we are teetering on self-extinction. We must really come to understand the shared nature of existence: nothing stands apart. Nothing exists outside the womb of limitless mutuality.

Albert Einstein made this point perfectly clear when he said: "Our separation from each other is an optical illusion of consciousness."

The more we *actually feel* our interrelated 'human nature' the more transparent the 'veils of separateness' become, the more we'll feel the joys and sorrows of others as our own.

Mother Teresa spoke to our inherent mutuality saying: "If we have no peace, it is because we have forgotten that we belong to each other."

One of the first things I learned living under conditions of tyranny — and yet one of the hardest lessons to actually manifest — was to simply listen and honor our *inherent mutuality*, in order to support and learn from those who were suffering, without being so self-involved as to try to heal or fix them.

To keep this truth close to my heart I would often recall a story of an Australian aboriginal woman. Approached by a white social worker, who said, rather presumptuously, "I'm here to help you. What can I do?" The woman replied, "If you're here to help me, please go. But if you see that my freedom and yours are linked, then please stay and we can serve each other."

"Our greatest need at the present time is perhaps for a global ethic, transcending all other systems of allegiance and belief — rooted in a consciousness of the interrelatedness and sanctity of all life."

~ **Federico Mayor, former Director-General of UNESCO**

30. ENNOBLING ACTION

"When we come face-to-face with the actualities of human and planetary suffering, what does the powerful moment of truth do to us?" Vimala Thakar asks. "Do we retreat into the comforts of theories and defense mechanisms, or are we awakened at the core of our being?"

*H*ow does the human heart open to such an extent that we feel the inherent bond of both freedom and suffering among us all? What wisdom awakens us at the core of our being to engage not just with our own immediate relationships but with all life? And further, how do we consciously evolve civilization as a whole, existence itself?

"The only thing that can save the world is the reclaiming of the awareness of the world."

~ Allen Ginsberg

"Individually and collectively, we are products of evolution," Tom Atlee, founder of the Institute for Co-intelligence, explains. "Evolution produced us through 13.7 billion years of trial and error and a few thousand years of more or less conscious choices by thousands of people we call our parents, leaders, elders, ancestors. ...And now we are the ones making choices that are shaping the evolution of the future — not only future generations of humanity but future generations of all life on earth. The question becomes: how conscious are we about who we are, what we are doing, where our motivations come from, and the consequences of the choices we make? Do we realize that our awareness, our intelligence, our desires and dreams, our creativity and efforts — seasoned by wisdom, or not — have become evolution, right here on earth, now?"

"We don't set out to save the world," Pema Chödrön explains. "We set out to wonder how other people are doing and to reflect on how our actions affect other people's hearts."

Here, the notion of *ubuntu*, a word rooted in South African culture, takes on a powerful and intimate meaning. "A person becomes human through other persons," Desmond Tutu explains. *Ubuntu* is the opposite of "I think, therefore I am." In other words, my humanness is inextricably bound up in yours. Such a person "does not feel threatened that others are able and good," he continues, "for he or she has a proper self-assurance that comes from knowing that he or she belongs in a greater whole, and is diminished when others are humiliated or diminished, when others are tortured or oppressed, or treated as if they were less than who they are."

Hasn't the time come to recognize the co-existence and co-creation of human destiny as self-evident fact? There have been such collective leaps before now. People once believed the Earth was flat, that the sun moved around a fixed planet. And that it was required as an individual, a nation-state, to own more possessions, control more people, have more extensive armed forces and weaponry, larger defense budgets and a vaster arsenal of terminally suicidal options for self-annihilation to pass as civilized.

Sounds like a myth? ...it is. Let us wake up from it!

After learning that the Indian government bought 66 Hawk fighter bombers from England, Arundhati Roy said, "Roughly, for the price of a single Hawk bomber, the government could provide one and a half million people with clean drinking water for life."

"To radically shift regime behavior we must think clearly and boldly for if we have learned anything, it is that regimes do not want to be changed. We must think beyond those who have gone before us, and discover technological changes that embolden us with ways to act in which our forebears could not. Firstly we must understand what aspect of government or neocorporatist behavior we wish to change or remove. Secondly we must develop a way of thinking about this behavior that is strong enough to carry us through the mire of politically distorted language, and into a position of clarity. Finally we must use these insights to inspire within us and others a course of ennobling, and effective action."

~ Julian Assange, "State and Terrorist Conspiracies"

31.   IN EACH OTHER

"We cannot live for ourselves alone. Our lives are connected by a thousand invisible threads, and along these sympathetic fibers, our actions run as causes and return to us as results."

~ Herman Melville

*A*s creatures born from the womb of infinite mutuality, the awakening of *a whole-world dharma* must be grounded in the discovery of our inherent unity. This requires examining the living-reality of our interpersonal awakening.

As Dr. Martin Luther King Jr. so famously acknowledged, "We are tied in a single garment of destiny. What affects one directly affects everyone indirectly." In other words, since we are always in a state of relatedness, dharma intelligence comes alive as we realize that freedom is never singular, and therefore, empower relationships as the most sacred place for awakening.

This expression of transformation is not about 'being here now with myself' alone, but being here now, together, so we grow and transform together.

What this means in contemporary, trans-spiritual terms is that by engaging relationships we discover ourselves. And in its more elevated meaning: By serving the freedom of others one frees oneself.

"We need the vision of *interbeing*," Thich Nhat Hanh
tells us. "We belong to each other; we cannot cut
reality into pieces. The well-being of 'this' is the
well-being of 'that,' so we have to do things together.
Every side is 'our side;' there is no evil side.

"One day we received a letter," Thich Nhat Hanh goes on to
explain, "telling us about a young girl on a small boat who
was raped by a Thai pirate. She was only twelve, and she
jumped into the ocean and drowned herself. When you first
learn of something like that, you get angry at the pirate. You
naturally take the side of the girl. As you look more deeply
you will see it differently. If you take the side of the little girl,
then it is easy. You only have to take a gun and shoot the
pirate. But we cannot do that."

Thich Nhat Hahn goes onto say, "In my meditation I saw that
if I had been born in the village of the pirate and raised in
the same conditions as he was, there is a great likelihood
that I would become a pirate. I saw that many babies are
born along the Gulf of Siam, hundreds every day, and if we
educators, social workers, politicians, and others do not do
something about the situation, in 25 years a number of them
will become sea pirates. That is certain. If you take a gun and
shoot the pirate, all of us are to some extent responsible for
this state of affairs."

"If we could read the secret history of our enemies,"
Henry Longfellow tells us, "we would find in
each man [and woman's] life a sorrow and a
suffering enough to disarm all hostility."

Can we look at each other and recognize
ourselves in each other?

"I am the mayfly metamorphosing on the surface of the river,"
Thich Nhat Hanh writes in his poem, *Call Me by My True Names*. "And I am the bird which, when spring comes, arrives in time to eat the mayfly. I am the child in Uganda, all skin and bones... and I am the arms merchant, selling...weapons to Uganda. I am the 12 year-old girl, refugee on a small boat, who throws herself into the ocean after being raped by a sea pirate, and I am the pirate, my heart not yet capable of seeing and loving." His words offer compelling reflection on the wisdom of *interbeing*, how we co-exist together in a "single fabric" of mutual destiny, diverse faces of the one mind, and the importance of transforming anger and blame into compassion and love.

"Deal with the faults of others as gently as with your own," states an ancient Chinese proverb. In other words "I have found that the more we care for the happiness of others, the greater is our own sense of well-being," asserts the 14th Dalai Lama. "Cultivating a close, warmhearted feeling for others puts the mind at ease. It helps remove whatever fears or insecurities we may have and gives us the strength to cope with any obstacles we encounter."

"While nothing is easier than the denounce the evildoer, nothing
is more difficult than to understand him."

~ Dostoevsky

Let us remember: our shared humanity is more
important than all the things that divide us.

32.   CREATIVELY ENGAGE

R. D. Laing once said, "The study of the experience of others, is based on inferences I make from my experience of you experiencing me, about how you are experiencing me experiencing you experiencing me. Social phenomenology is the science of 'my own and of others' experience. It is concerned with the relation between my experience of you and your experience of me. That is, with *inter-experience*. It is concerned with your behavior and my behavior as I experience it, and your and my behavior as you experience it."

The more intimately we understand our inherent inter-relatedness we see how life-transformation would not be possible without each other. In other words, we cannot become free in isolation. How could one cultivate generosity without other life to give to? How could one cultivate compassion without opening one's eyes to those who are suffering? How would one ever know the value of integrity unless there was a context to see it contrasted with deception?

Thus, to make relationships our vehicle to awaken one attempts what the traditional Buddhist texts suggest: 'Make each person you meet your ultimate object of reverence.'

"Reverence awakens in the soul a sympathetic power," Rudolf Steiner states, "through which we attract qualities in the beings around us, which would otherwise remain concealed."

Nelson Mandela expressed the challenge of empowering relationships as the source of liberating-awakening by saying:

"Do I believe people are good at their core? There is no doubt whatsoever, provided you are able to arouse that goodness inherent in every human. Those of us in the fight against apartheid changed many people who hated us because they discovered that we respected them."

"I go and talk to another man," Robert Anton Wilson tells us. "He is experienced deeply part of the time, and shallowly another part of the time, depending on the quality of my consciousness. If I am very conscious, meeting him can be an experience comparable to great music or even an earthquake. If I am in the usual shallow state, however, he barely makes an impression.

"If I am practicing alertness and neurological self-criticism," he goes into say, "I may observe that I am only experiencing him part of the time, and that part of the time I am not-tuning-in but drifting off to my favorite "Real" universe and editing out at the ear-drum much of what he is saying. Often, the "Real" universe hypnotizes me sufficiently that, while I "hear" what he says, I have no idea of the way he says it or what he means to convey."

To 'revere others' we must first listen to them, hear what they are actually saying. With such respect we bring our most conscientious qualities of heart to the forefront with others and creatively engage shared space.

"From entering the intelligence of 'conscious mutuality,' higher potentials emerge. By liberating our intimacy, a new closeness offers finer textures of tenderness, and more opportunities for heightened synergy."

~ Jeannine Davies

As we relax ego-centric individualism and fear-driven isolation, we become devoted to life, and not to dogmatic theories that insidiously separate us from it. From such an open and vital space of being we can co-create a new order of feeling, an experience of shared life perhaps never before known on earth.

Open the windows of your heart.
Engage your neighbors — creatively, generously.

"Won't you come into the garden? I would like my roses to see you."

~ **Richard Brinsley Sheridan**

33.   EVERYONE

> "The true person is not anyone in particular but, like the deep blue color
> of the limitless sky, it is everyone, everywhere in the world."
>
> ~ Do-gen Zenji

*L*ife experience is our greatest teacher and therefore the most genuine space for awakening.

It is awareness that illuminates and liberates, not a teacher, nor a doctrine, nor a form.

I would like to extend that essential understanding by saying life experience is *lived experience*. We don't just sit by the side of the river and watch it go by.

The point is to immerse oneself in it. In reality, there is no place one can stand to be outside of life looking in at it, no matter how we might try.

We are life.
Life is us.
I am my relationships.
My relationships are me.

We are alive within a whole universe of interrelated life.

> "Life does not exist on Earth's surface, so much as it is Earth's surface."
>
> ~ Lynn Margulis and Dorian Sagan

"Because reality is dependently co-arising, or systemic in nature," writes Buddhist scholar, author, and teacher Joanna Macy, "each and every act is understood to have an effect on the larger web of life, and the process of development is perceived as multidimensional. One's personal awakening is integral to the awakening of one's village and both play integral roles in the awakening of one's country and world."

As Carl Sandburg so beautifully expressed:

"There is only one man in the world
And his name is All Men.

There is only one woman in the world
And her name is All Women.

There is only one child in the world
And the child's name is All Children."

"Another world is not only possible, she is on her way. On a quiet day, if you listen carefully, you can hear her breathing."

~ Arundhati Roy

34. HUMAN MIRRORS

"The human is a space, an opening, where the universe celebrates
its experience."

~ Brian Swimme

*O*ne of my most durable memories of co-creative intimacy came years ago when I lived in Bali. One day my friend invited a friend of hers to visit. When the friend arrived at the house, she had brought her brother along. When they walked in I noticed he had trouble with his eyes. They looked empty. She explained that Wayan was blind and that he had been unable to see since birth.

After some tea she and my friend took a walk, leaving me and Wayan on the veranda. After a few minutes of sitting together in silence I noticed that he was smiling. I asked him why? "Your house is in the country, isn't it?" he responded.

"Yes, it's on the side of a gorge."

"I can feel it," he said. "This is very soothing to me. I live in a one-room apartment in the city. Thank you for having me here." He paused for a few moments, and with his smile growing deeper and more reflective, he asked, "May I ask you a question?"

"Sure," I said.

"Would you take me around your home and describe what you see? I'd like to enjoy your home the way you see it and enjoy it. In Bali we say that we get to know a person by *how they see the world.*" I was deeply touched by his invitation. It was so pure.

"Sure," I said. "I'd be honored."

I took him by the hand and we stood up and began to slowly walk around the house. I took him to a Buddha statue that had been sitting on an altar over the table for years but as I tried to describe it to him, I realized he hadn't asked me to give him a visual tour of things alone, but what I enjoyed about these things, how I felt about them, what my relationship was with them.

I found myself sharing half-truths, fragmented stories without their complete meaning. He was not asking me to feel sorry for him or to say something that might entertain him.

He was inviting me to reveal my heart, to be honest and tender to the truth of my experience. It was the oddest thing to realize how inward I had been and how much of my day-to-day environment I had never really noticed, nor really understood or enjoyed. My relatedness to life was selective and somewhat narrow and perfunctory.

"The general idea is that if you open yourself to what the given situation is, then you see its completely naked quality. You don't have to put up a defense mechanism anymore, because you see through it and you know exactly what to do.

You just deal with things, rather than defending yourself."

~ Chögyam Trungpa

When I took him to the upstairs living room I caught a glimpse of myself in the large mirror against one wall. I wasn't sure where to begin. He picked up my hesitation and said, "If I am disturbing you I can sit alone until my sister returns." I assured him I was deciding on what to tell him next. He then said in an inviting tone, "May I ask, what do you look like?" My heart quivered.

There was something so utterly transparent about this man. While he sat in a chair I looked in the mirror and described myself to him. Although he was blind, he was skilled in bringing vision to light. His profound awareness allowed him, in spite of his injured eyes, to grasp the sensual details of the material world. Instead of continuing to take my own sight for granted, he reminded me what my own eyes see and do. It was also as if his blindness showed me my own — a metaphysical perception, just as disabling and far-reaching, if not more so, than his mere lack of sight.

Overall, he brought me into a much more nuanced intimacy through our uninhibited expressions of shared presence.

"We do not really see ourselves. All mirrors are in fact quite useless except the living, human mirrors who reflect us: They do not lie."

~ Francois Mauriac

Honor all wounds, as well as strengths, in oneself and others. In them might be the healing that brings us closer to each other.

35.   US RIGHT NOW

> "A dream you dream alone is only a dream.
> A dream you dream together is reality."
>
> ~ John Lennon

*A*ll ways of opening the heart prepare us for the liberating intimacy of us right now. This points to the participatory intelligence that on the one hand honors our uniqueness and on the other respects that we are in relationship to everything all the time.

As freedom becomes more important than safety, the heart grows stronger and less protective, and we become more available to actually participate in intimate situations. As such, we don't abandon ourselves to interrelate with others. We awaken to the already present reality of where we meet the world and the world meets us — with the senses, with the mind, with the flesh of our body; self with subselves, self with others, self with heart and world.

> "The consciousness of loving and being loved brings a warmth
> and richness to life that nothing else can bring."
>
> ~ Oscar Wilde

As a result of this recognition, the psychologist Jeannine Davies states, "We bring our most intuitive intelligence to the inter-subjective canvas of mutual-being on which we co-create original existence."

Whenever I have consciously created from within this space of mutual belonging I have learned the greatest life lessons. It is where I have broken open, awakened, fallen in love, and co-created a child. It has brought me closer to myself and others in ways that I never dreamt possible.

"But here they were shedding skins. They could imitate nothing but what they were. There was no defense but to look for the truth in each other."

~ **Michael Ondaatje**

36.   PRESENCE

"Happiness is when what you think, what you say,
and what you do are in harmony."

~ **Mahatma Gandhi**

*O**ur* presence is all we have.
We take it with us wherever we go.

Situate your heart close to others.
Although intimacy poses challenges, counter them.
Attune yourself to shared space.

Listen with all of your senses.
Learn from your own shortcomings.
Elevate yourself and others with goodness.

Transmute negativity with its positive opposite:
transform fear with courage; anger with love;
greed with giving; restlessness with patience.

Bring hope to people through your actions.
Remember: Our presence is all we have.

Carl Rogers, in describing the essence of presence, said:
"Being genuine is the willingness to be and to express, in
words and behavior, the various feelings and attitudes which
exist in you. It is only in this way that the relationship can
have reality... — be real."

"Can one be spiritual without religious faith?" Elie Wiesel asks. "One can. All one needs is to be open to someone else's concerns, fears, and hopes, and make him or her feel less alone, less abandoned...It is my caring for the otherness in others that determines my humanity. And my spirituality."

> "I believe the greatest gift I can conceive of having from anyone is to be seen by them, heard by them, to be understood and touched by them."
>
> ~ Virginia Satir

37.   ORIGINAL EXISTENCE

"Either you think — or else others have to think for you
and take power from you, pervert and discipline your natural
tastes, civilize and sterilize you."

~ F. Scott Fitzgerald

Embrace experience — your own unique human experience — mindful of the interplay of life at the confluence of the inner and outer. Create your life from a naked *nirvana*; avoid filtering it through mythification, consensus reality or the propaganda of certainty. From this dynamic, unburdened by the armor of pretense or blame, enter this moment now as the playground of original existence and evolve your highest potential.

Improvise your life within and
beyond the global mindscape.
Be experimental.
Roam the edges.
Elevate.
Breathe more fully.
Imagine the unimaginable.
Be, all that you are and want to be.

Robert Pirsig wrote in *Zen and the Art of Motorcycle Maintenance,* "We take a handful of sand from the endless landscape of awareness around us and call that handful of sand the world."

Rethink the world. Take one hundred handfuls of sand. Challenge the assumptions behind the assumptions.

> "The real risks for any artist are taken in pushing the work to the limits of what is possible."
>
> **~ Salman Rushdie**

Look at it this way: awareness is an 'always now' dynamic. In that sense, there can never be enough awareness. Yet being present isn't the end of all the *dharma life*. Awareness must be linked with other liberating qualities of consciousness. In other words: awareness supports one waking up from the trance of habit — the mind sees and feels itself; you are no longer asleep. Imagination is the intuitive flash of possibility illuminating your originality, your unexpressed vision. And *dharma intelligence* is the liberating force that creatively arouses you to undertake every action necessary to manifest your innermost dreams, while caring for the freedom of others.

> "Freedom of expression is the matrix, the indispensable condition, of nearly every form of freedom."
>
> **~ Benjamin Cardozo**

Lowry Burgess, the pioneering artist who created the first official art payload taken into outer space by NASA in 1989, when asked to describe his sculpture that was part of the payload, explained: "I gathered water from the mouths of the 18 greatest rivers in the world...distilled them into pure water on the surface of the Dead Sea, then worked with chemists to add all the elements in the periodic table. Then ... placed that water inside a cube that was...inside [another] cube. The inner cube was a vacuum chamber, which floats in the water in the outer cube — so the "everything" surrounds the "nothing".... The whole concept of the work required zero gravity. It's about the release of everything and nothing into floating freedom: weightlessness."

Albert Einstein once asked himself, "What would I see in a mirror if I were traveling as fast as light?"

Locate your zero gravity, your weightlessness, your most free flowing sense of freedom, and imagine: there is nothing that you cannot do.

"The only way to discover the limits of the possible
is to go beyond them into the impossible."
~ Arthur C. Clarke

38.   VICTORY

"The life of God — the life which the mind apprehends and enjoys as it rises to the absolute unity of all things — may be described as a play of love with itself; but this idea sinks to an edifying truism, or even to a platitude, when it does not embrace in it the earnestness, the pain, the patience, and labor, involved in the negative aspect of things."

~ G.W.F. Hegel

*A*s humans, we live in a world not of our making. We're forced, if you will, by biological nature to participate in our own existence. By necessity we are compelled to eat, drink, and interrelate — but the intensity and contradiction pressed onto human experience can grow unimaginably dark. It's nearly impossible to hold our hearts open while imagining the daily existence of a child prostitute, or a teenager strung out on crack or crystal meth, wasting away on some city street or in a suburban locked-in room of alienation and self-defeat. Or what it must be like to be one of the hundreds of wrongly accused awaiting execution on America's death row. Or to feel the anguish of one of the tens-of-thousands of returning soldiers suffering acute trauma from the horrors of engagement in wrongful wars. Or the unspeakable torment of the two million girls subjected to genital mutilation each year.

It's no wonder so many people find it so difficult to embrace life here on earth as to engage their humanness in seeking a so-called better life beyond this world, following religions and spiritual paths that espouses escape from this torment. A compassionate response to ignorance and suffering understands our human drive toward escape. But to resist the desire to escape, to embrace the many faces of reality, requires the heart to transform the darkness, sometimes by just feeling it.

"I learned that courage was not the absence of fear, but the triumph over it. I felt fear more times than I can remember, but I hid it behind a mask of boldness. The brave man is not he who does not feel afraid, but he who conquers fear."

~ Nelson Mandela

"Victory, in this struggle with the powers of darkness," Bertrand Russell once said, "is the true baptism into the glorious company of heroes, the true initiation into the overmastering beauty of human existence. From that Awful encounter of the soul with the outer world, renunciation, wisdom, and charity are born; and with their birth a new life begins. To take into the inmost shrine of the soul the irresistible forces whose puppets we seem to be — death and change, the irrevocableness of the past, and the powerlessness of man before the blind hurry of the universe from vanity to vanity — to feel these things and know them is to conquer them."

"Keep me away from the wisdom which does not cry, the philosophy which does not laugh, and the greatness which does not bow before children."

~ Kahlil Gibran

39.   GOOD AND EVIL

"From pacifist to terrorist, each person condemns violence — and then
adds one cherished case in which it may be justified."

~ Gloria Steinem

*W*here does darkness come from? Is there, in fact, intrinsic evil? Do we all fight an archetypal repository of demonic energy, which at any moment could spew hell and oppression through the unmindful crevices of our psyches?

Is there really a mind without conscience, a psychopath, a killer in everyone, who could be triggered by unforeseen circumstances?

And if so, from where does this wickedness arise?

From sexual repression?

Humankind's irrational drive for domination and power?

A tortured childhood?

A blueprint from birth?

From the genetics of our reptilian past?

Or is it karma — an ancient (re)-action contorting one's behavior?

Or are we in a cold universe without true meaning?

Whatever the source, the conditions are clear: suffering exists! And human beings for one reason or another perpetuate the torment with enormous fervor and conviction.

Am I exempt?

Am I beyond the possibility of an act of violence that from another perspective is an "act of evil?"

"There have been periods of history in which episodes of terrible violence occurred but for which the word violence was never used," writes Gil Bailie in his book *Violence Unveiled*. "Violence is shrouded in justifying myths that lend it moral legitimacy, and these myths for the most part kept people from recognizing the violence for what it was. The people who burned witches at the stake never for one moment thought of their act as violence; rather they thought of it as an act of divinely mandated righteousness. The same can be said of most of the violence we humans have ever committed."

Doubtless, there is evil in the world. How and why this darkness exists is beyond our comprehension, so it seems. What we do know is that the human heart is not sectioned into black-and-white regions of pure good and absolute bad. We are not living in a world with only two kinds of people: the right ones — us, and the wrong ones — them.

Aleksandr Solzhenitsyn once said, "If only it were all so simple. If only there were evil people somewhere insidiously committing evil deeds, and it were necessary only to separate them from the rest of us and destroy them. But the line dividing good and evil cuts through the heart of every human being. And who is willing to destroy a piece of his own heart?"

"Peace is not the absence of conflict; it's the absence of violence within conflict."

~ Claude Anshin Thomas

40. OWN YOUR SHADOW

"The purpose of thinking about the future is not to predict it but to raise people's hopes."

~ Freeman Dyson, Physicist at Princeton's Institute for Advanced Study

The future of civilization is linked to our ability to overcome the forces of ignorance both internal and external to ourselves. Despite the fact that we are handicapped by biological constraints — brains hard-wired to prompt irrationality, rage, and violence — we must innovatively challenge our most primitive urges. Genetically (and psychically) passed on to us through an ancient legacy of ancestry, these reptilian 'up-surges' are effectively obsolete.

It's crucial that we do all that we can to limit their eruption within the psyche and their spillover into the world. We must learn the wisdom of transforming these primal forces and hope that in time we overcome and outgrow these traits, so that they can gradually disappear from the collective gene pool and leave the template of consciousness altogether.

Of course, deprogramming the mind of hostility and irrationality, and reconfiguring it toward kindness and tolerance, is an ancient ideal. Today, such ambitions are no longer confined to spiritual, philosophical, and psychological circles. The harsh realities of even our most recent history have shown us how just a few people with hostile fantasies can rain hell down on the multitude. The need to identify the forces giving rise to every form of human and environmental degradation has never been greater.

"Violence is the last refuge of the incompetent."

~ Isaac Asimov

Look at it this way. Each of us is essentially a gorgeous mystery with a wild heart and a lofty purpose. But within each of us, without exception, the psyche harbors a segment of the world's psychosis: an inner theater of repressed symbols injected with primordial hatreds, enervating wounds, and undiscovered powers. The 'great unconscious' has been known by many names; darkness, the Devil, evil, and stupidity. Carl Jung called it "the human shadow" — those emotional traits that we despise, disown, and repress and live buried in the darkness of our subconscious minds, safe from our judgments. Yet it is always there, waiting to be triggered into unconscious projection anywhere, anytime.

In offering his finest advice on what each of us can do to change the world Jung stated: "The best political, social, and spiritual work we can do is to withdraw the projection of our shadow onto others."

In other words, as Nietzsche said, "The great epochs in our lives are at the points when we gain the courage to rebaptize our badness as the best in us."

"To fall out of grace is one of the greatest gifts that one receives in life," states Sobonfu Somé. "When we are in grace, we begin to take things for granted and we actually stop working on ourselves. Falling out of grace shakes us up. It reconnects us to the larger universe in order for us to see ourselves anew. It forces us to rediscover where our true center begins and learn what needs to be set aside."

"My heroes are the ones who survived doing it wrong, who made mistakes, but recovered from them," Bono once said. And they kept on "walking on."

And it was Gandhi who said "the victory is in the struggle itself."

The struggle itself is the most important thing.

And no matter what, keep on summoning the courage to walk on — reclaiming your own shadow and rebaptizing it as the best in you.

> "Emancipate yourself from mental slavery, none but ourselves can free our mind."
>
> ~ Bob Marley

41.　　GRASPING THE ROOT

"Revolution, in order to be creative must have a moral or metaphysical
rule to balance the insanity of history."

~ Albert Camus

*S*omeone once asked the Dalai Lama why he didn't fight
back against the Chinese? He replied, "War is obsolete, you
know. Of course the mind can rationalize fighting back... but
the heart... would never understand....you would be divided
in yourself...and the war would be inside you."

"Nonviolence means avoiding not only external physical violence but
also internal violence of spirit. You not only refuse to shoot a man,
but you refuse to hate him."

~ Martin Luther King, Jr.

What is most urgently needed in the world today?

A revolution in the sphere of human consciousness occurs
only when we learn how to challenge our own fear, anger,
and ignorance, leading the way towards lasting change
and peace. Aung San Suu Kyi and the people of her country
introduced me to this style of revolution. In Burma, the
nonviolent struggle for freedom to overcome dictatorship is
known as a 'revolution of the spirit.' It is a revolution rooted
in the wisdom of honesty, immediacy and radical self-
responsibility. In other words, by facing the truth in oneself
— by empowering one's own conscience — one is in the best
position to act from love and compassion rather than from
fear and revenge.

> "Returning violence for violence multiplies violence, adding deeper darkness to a night already devoid of stars. Darkness cannot drive out hate; only love can do that."
>
> ~ **Martin Luther King, Jr.**

"Soon after the Gulf War happened I made some pledge or resolution," the 14th Dalai Lama states, "that the rest of my life will be committed to the demilitarization of the planet."

Can we make this same pledge?

"I refuse to accept the view that mankind is so tragically bound to the starless midnight of racism and war that the bright daybreak of peace and brotherhood can never become reality," Martin Luther King, Jr. once said. "I believe that unarmed truth and unconditional love will have the final word."

An elder Cherokee Native American was teaching his grandchildren about life, the legend goes. He said to them, "A fight is going on inside me; it is a terrible fight, and it is between two wolves. One wolf represents fear, anger, greed, arrogance, guilt, inferiority, lies, and superiority. The other wolf stands for joy, love, hope, humility, kindness, empathy, generosity, truth and compassion. This same fight is going on inside of you and every other person too." They thought about it for a minute and then one child asked his grandfather, "Which wolf will win?" The grandfather replied, "The one I feed."

> "Radical simply means 'grasping things at the root."
>
> ~ **Angela Davis**

42.   PRACTICE IT

"None are more hopelessly enslaved than those who falsely believe
they are free."

~ Goethe

*T*o hope that the *dharma life* — our quest for liberation —
will fully alleviate inner complexity or bring unconditional
freedom is an alluring but erroneous hope. No one has
completely divested themselves of the inherent delusions
within the psyche. No one is abiding in an Absolute state
of perfect psychological or existential harmony. No one
has completely uprooted the afflictive emotions of anger,
ignorance, and greed. No one is beyond suffering; no matter
how 'liberated' they may appear. Consciousness is simply too
vast and complex to fully explore and wisely understand at
this point in human evolution.

But we must try.

"And so, to the end of history, murder shall breed murder, always in
the name of right and honor and peace, until the gods are tired of
blood and create a race that can understand."

~ George Bernard Shaw

Could there be anything more important than to tame the
savageness of man, to end the cycle of human cruelty, man's
inhumanity to man?

"I don't believe that ...politicians and the capitalists alone are guilty of the war," Anne Frank wrote in her diary. "There is an urge and rage in people to destroy, to kill, to murder, and until all mankind, without exception, undergoes a great change, wars will be waged." And that means 'everybody.'

Paulo Freire writes that even "the oppressed suffer from the duality which has established itself in their innermost being. They discover that without freedom they cannot exist authentically. Yet, although they desire authentic existence, they fear it. They are at one and the same time themselves and the oppressor whose consciousness they have internalized."

"Monsters exist, but they are too few in number to be truly dangerous," Primo Levi informs us. "More dangerous are the common men, the functionaries ready to believe and to act without asking questions."

"If you want the present to be different from the past, study the past."

~ Spinoza

"The distance we feel from our actions is proportionate to our ignorance of them," writes the philosopher John Lachs. "Our ignorance, in turn, is largely a measure of the length of the chain of intermediaries between ourselves and our acts. As consciousness of the context drops out," he continues, "the actions become motions without consequence. With the consequence out of view, people can be parties to the most horrific acts without raising the question of their own role and responsibility. Wage earners who insert the fuse in bombs can then view their activity as but a series of repetitive motions performed for a living. Railroad workers who take trainloads of prisoners to extermination camps can think of themselves as simply providing transportation."

"The reasonable man adapts himself to the world," explains George Bernard Shaw. "The unreasonable one persists in trying to adapt the world to himself. Therefore, all progress depends on the unreasonable man."

As Vaclav Havel states, "[We] should constantly disturb," the basis for persisting in one's commitment to a 'non-adaptive freedom' and an 'unreasonable wisdom.'

"[We] should bear witness to the misery of the world," he goes on to say. "[We] should be provocative by being independent; should rebel against all hidden and open pressures and manipulations; should be the chief doubter of systems, of power and its incantations; and should be a witness to their mendacity. For this very reason...[we] essentially don't belong anywhere; [we] stand out as an irritant wherever [we are]..."

"We must be free not because we claim freedom, but because we *practice it*."

~ William Faulkner

43.   FIND NEW FORMS

The revolution of consciousness and the transformation of the world will not be won or lost in a city street, in cyberspace, or in the halls of power alone. It will happen on the front lines of the human heart — that stormy region of good and evil, genius and madness, peace and war, battle for dominion over conscience, freedom, and love.

> To take freedom as our life's purpose is
> clearly one of the greatest of challenges.

It means making the terrible beautiful and kissing each heartbreak as Divinity itself.

Become an "Angel-headed hipster" Allen Ginsberg howled, "burning for the ancient heavenly connection to the starry dynamo in the machinery of night."

In other words, "Accept [your] reality as vastly as [you] possibly can," Rainer Maria Rilke encourages us. "Everything, even the unprecedented, must be possible within it. This is in the end the only kind of courage that is required of us: the courage to face the strangest, most unusual, most inexplicable experiences that can beset us."

Easier said than done.

Why?

"We are at odds with ourselves internally," explains Vimala Thakar. "We believe that the inner is fundamentally different from the outer, that what is me is quite separate from the not-me, that divisions among people and nations are necessary, and yet we wonder why there are tensions, conflicts, wars in the world. The conflicts begin with the mind that believes in fragmentation and is ignorant of wholeness."

> "Believe nothing merely because you have been told it. Do not believe what your teacher tells you simply out of respect for the teacher. But whatsoever, after critical analysis, and intuitive reflection, you find to be kind, conducive to the good of all beings — believe that doctrine, actualize it and take it as your guide."
>
> **~ The Buddha**

Tom Atlee explains the "six facets of wholeness": "1) *Unity* includes anything that holds a whole together, that makes it one thing. 2) *Diversity* provides options, resources and stimulation; it generates vitality and evolution. 3) *Relationship* connects people and things, events and possibilities, ideas and images, linking or weaving them together. 4) *Uniqueness* means that everyone, everything, every moment has qualities possessed by no other person, thing or moment. 5) *Context* is what's around us — the conditions, forces, structures and mindsets that contain what's going on, that shape it and give it meaning. 6) *Interiority* is what's inside us — the generative center out of which awareness, resourcefulness, motivation and many other phenomena arise."

And why is wholeness important? From the recognition of our inseparable unity, our inherent human-environmental relatedness, we bring evolution to consciousness. Tom Atlee goes on to explain this point saying, "The fact of evolution means we are all related. Not just we humans, but all entities in the universe — all are expressions of one universe. We have been kin since the infinitely intense birth of this universe, when we were obviously one but not separate enough to notice the fact. We all arose from the Source of that — whatever that may have been — and we are all made of stardust, literally. Two hundred million generations ago, our ancestors swam in the sea; today the chemistry of the sea flows through our veins. Our bodies contain great civilizations of highly specialized and synchronized single-celled beings, cousins of the trillions of microbes that populate the world around us. All humanity is one family, rich with diversity yet sharing one root. Deep inside we know this, we resonate with one another, we are drawn into relationship, support, and celebration. Love is not something that needs to be added or built, only freed and nurtured, for it is our natural state. On the other hand, evolution is about moving from old states of wholeness into new states of wholeness. So love can and must *find new forms* and ways to be and do."

"You cannot get through a single day without having an impact on the world around you. What you do makes a difference, and you have to decide what kind of difference you want to make."

~ Jane Goodall

44.   THE FORCE OF LOVE

"Reconnect with the spiritual force that animates the best in you. Then let
your every action flow from your strength and compassion."

~ Fran Korten

*T*ransforming human suffering is a complex and largely
mysterious affair. I have a dear friend, a skilled psychotherapist
whose expertise is in working with sexual violence against
women, and the resulting trauma. In reflecting on her years
of working in the Balkans, Afghanistan, and Darfur with
victims of war, she admitted that there was no single method
or process to help someone liberate him- or herself from the
horror, the trauma, and the pain. The most effective way, she
said, was "simply being there — showing up, sitting in tender
silence, often crying together, just being sisters of the heart."

"Awareness of misery, without defense structures, will naturally lead
to action. The heart cannot witness misery without calling the being
into action, without activating *the force of love.*"

~ Vimala Thakar

"Eventually, if and when the tears subsided," she went
onto say, "I would encourage the women to see if they
could feel the 'healing magic of contribution' — helping
each other restore their sense of worth and confidence, by
'giving back and to each other' in whatever way they felt
was real and right. These heroic women refused to settle for
bitterness alone."

They transformed the most incomprehensible edges of life's madness, and "in so doing, many of the women," she concluded, "became even stronger and wiser than ever before."

> "Out of suffering have emerged the strongest souls; the most massive characters are seared with scars."
>
> ~ **Kahlil Gibran**

45. ACT — TAKE SIDES!

"Truth is not only violated by falsehood; it may be outraged by silence."

~ Henri Frédéric Amiel

*A*ung San Suu Kyi once said, "Fearlessness may be a gift but perhaps more precious is the courage acquired through endeavor, courage that comes from cultivating the habit of refusing to let fear dictate one's actions, courage that could be described as grace under pressure — grace which is renewed repeatedly in the face of harsh, unremitting pressure."

Thus, each person has to confront their fear.

It takes courage to lift up one's eyes from their needs and to see the truth of the world around them — a truth, such as in Burma, where 'speaking out for freedom will land you in prison.'

It takes courage not to turn away; not to make excuses for non-involvement; and not to be corrupted by cynicism or fear. It takes courage to feel one's own conscience; because once you do you must enter your heart, your integrity, your dignity, your worth as a human being: you must engage your fundamental purpose for being alive.

"The true revolutionary is guided by a great feeling of love. It is impossible to think of a genuine revolutionary lacking this quality."

~ Ernesto Che Guevara

And if you are to empower the "great feeling of love" — the self-respect to act on behalf of your conscience — you must confront every obstacle, real or imagined, that suggests inaction is preferable to action. Because we can't just expect to sit idly by and have freedom handed to us.

Liberation cannot be achieved this way.

It will be successful only when everyone realizes they can do their part.

> In this regard, Aung San Suu Kyi said that "courage is three-fold: The courage to see. The courage to feel. And the courage to act. If all three domains are realized our revolution will succeed."

"The regime's use of mass arrests, murder, torture, and imprisonment has failed to extinguish our desire for the freedom that was stolen from us," said the Burmese Buddhist monk U Gambira, a leader of the nationwide pro-democracy demonstrations in September 2007, now serving a 65 year prison sentence.

"Now it is the generals who must fear the consequences of their actions," he continues. "We adhere to nonviolence, but our spine is made of steel. There is no turning back. It matters little if my life or the lives of colleagues should be sacrificed on this journey. Others will fill our sandals, and more will join and follow," he concludes.

"I swore never to be silent whenever and wherever human beings endure suffering and humiliation. We must always *take sides*. Neutrality helps the oppressor, never the victim. Silence encourages the tormentor, never the tormented."

~ **Elie Wiesel**

46. BEAUTY

Dostoyevsky once said, "Beauty will save the world."
But what is this beauty that will save the world?

*B*eauty is so many things. It's an emotion. It's a way of seeing, feeling, and being. To be stirred in one's heart is beautiful. It's beautiful to see courage triumph over adversity. To feel someone's solidarity with our own struggle is beautiful. Kindness and gratitude are beautiful. Dear friendship is beautiful. Feeling the intimate nature of our interdependent-existence is beautiful. Knowing that we can love and be loved is beautiful.

Nurturing a child is beautiful. Having the confidence that we can transform our lives is beautiful. Living from within the depth of our values is beautiful. As is standing up for truth, freedom and global human rights. Reconciliation and mutual forgiveness are beautiful. Gazing into infinity is beautiful. Singing with your child is beautiful. As is a smile, a song, a photograph, and a memory of love. And perhaps, having a generous nature may be the finest beauty of all.

Why?

Because we cannot live without each other. Literally.

Aung San Suu Kyi explains what it means to have 'a generous nature,' saying: "It is a noble nature. A kind nature that is loving and giving and forgiving. A nature that rejoices in the good fortune of others and allows for the weaknesses of others in a true spirit of humility that recognizes one's own weaknesses. It is a nature that seeks to alleviate the sufferings of others; not to aggravate them with self-righteous condemnation or ruthless aggression. It is a nature in which there is little room for jealousy or covetousness or contempt. It is a nature that is warm and caring. At this point, perhaps, I should hasten to say that I am not talking about saints, I am simply talking of the kind of people who can help to make our life a little happier in spite of the unavoidable trials and tribulations of worldly existence."

"The final forming of a person's character lies in their own hands."

~ **Anne Frank**

47.   WHEN YOU ARE RIGHT

> "The greatest triumphs of propaganda have been accomplished, not by doing something, but by refraining from doing. Great is truth, but still greater, from a practical point of view, is silence about truth."
>
> ~ **Aldous Huxley**

"*All* human beings, whatever their cultural or historical background, suffer when they are intimidated, imprisoned or tortured," the 14th Dalai Lama states. "We must, therefore, insist on a global consensus, not only on the need to respect human rights worldwide, but also on the definition of these rights ... for it is the inherent nature of all human beings to yearn for freedom, equality and dignity, and they have an equal right to achieve that."

"Where, after all, do universal human rights begin?" Eleanor Roosevelt invites us to consider. "In small places, close to home — ...Unless [they]...have meaning there, they have little meaning anywhere."

Could there be anything more sacred, more important than the wisdom that manifests global freedom, the human right to co-exist in peace, free of fear, and free of want? Take away someone's most basic freedoms, and generally speaking, they suffer the greatest loss. For me, to not be able to move about freely, or to speak openly, or to voice my dissent, for fear of imprisonment, confiscation of property, or harm to myself or my family, is unimaginable.

Nelson Mandela said that during the twenty-seven years he spent largely in Robben Island prison "I thought continually of the day when I would walk free." He proclaims freedom as the highest good — a quality so immeasurable that no fear was too large to confront in ending apartheid. Not the fear of torture, or even of death, would stand in the way of his commitment. "Our message," he declared, "was that no sacrifice was too great in the struggle for freedom."

"When you are right you cannot be too radical."

~ Martin Luther King, Jr.

"We were not frightened. We thought the worst thing the Chinese could do was either kill us or put us in prison. We were already prepared to give up our lives for the six million Tibetans," said Ngawang Phulchung, a Buddhist monk who spent nearly two decades in prison for protests against China's occupation of his country and other 'crimes' that included printing copies of the

Universal Declaration of Human Rights
Universal Declaration of Human Rights
Universal Declaration of Human Rights
Universal Declaration of Human Rights.
Universal Declaration of Human Rights
Universal Declaration of Human Rights
Universal Declaration of Human Rights
Universal Declaration of Human Rights
Universal Declaration of Human Rights

Universal Declaration of Human Rights

that states "the inherent dignity and the equal and inalienable rights of all members of the human family is the foundation of freedom, justice and peace in the world."

"Human rights are the only ideology that deserves to survive."

~ **Simon Wiesenthal**

48. DIVE IN

Activating dharma intelligence is a liberating engagement of direct experience that always arises right now — at the windows of our perception. From such an awakened state of immediacy, live boldly — elevate and beautify life; frolic and make love with it.

Whatever excites your imagination,
Be you — eccentric, satirical, multitudinous.

"Artistic sensibility is the capacity to make the invisible visible by embracing the marginal, the perverse, the excluded."

~ Carlos Fuentes

Embrace your flawed human wholeness and live outwardly from there, such that your life "revives and readapts time and space," as Leonard Bernstein once said, and "lets you breathe its strange, special air."

And let us remember the importance of George Santayana's words, in honor of our failings (at times), of a life dedicated to transforming the 'imperfect present': "Unless you're ashamed of yourself now and then, you're not honest."

"Mistakes are the portals of discovery."

~ James Joyce

Dive in completely.

Participate fully by giving your gifts
and putting your talents to the highest use.

"The only treasure that survives after death is all that we have given."

~ **Aymara oral tradition**

49. CHANGING OUR WAYS

"Every man has three characters: that which he exhibits,
that which he has, that which he thinks he has."

~ Franz Kafka

*C*hallenging negative personal patterns requires bravery, honesty, and insight. It's the rare individual who wants to change by reclaiming projection, investigate the ignorance that propels it, and evolve their wiser, more compassionate self as sovereign over the state of their own mind and life. "We habitually erect a barrier called blame," Pema Chödrön states, citing this 'accusatory state of consciousness' as one of the central forces that prevents one from taking responsibility for the self-generated nature of one's inner life.

"[Blame also] ...keeps us from communicating genuinely with others," she goes on to say, "and we fortify it with our concepts of who's right and who's wrong. We [often] do that with the people who are closest to us and we do it with political systems, with all kinds of things that we don't like about our associates or our society. It's a very common, ancient, well-perfected device for trying to feel better — BLAME OTHERS. It is a way to protect your heart, trying to protect what is soft and open and tender in yourself. Rather than own that pain, we scramble to find some comfortable ground."

"We cannot change anything unless we accept it. Condemnation does not liberate," Carl Jung informs us, "it oppresses."

Liberate: To set free, as from oppression, confinement, or aberrant control.

"Compassionate action starts with seeing yourself when you start to make yourself right and when you start to make yourself wrong," Pema Chödrön continues. "At that point you could just contemplate the fact that there is a larger alternative to either of those, a more tender, shaky kind of place where you could live."

Compassion is actualized through choice.
It becomes real through choice.

And for compassion to become a revolutionary source of power we must learn as Aung San Suu Kyi counsels to "choose freedom" — inhabit your courage, face yourself, and no matter what, she concludes, "Act despite the fear."

Act despite any kind of fear; the fear of feeling your own vulnerability; the fear of losing control; the fear of being blamed, humiliated or abandoned; or the fear of feeling your own self-worth, your own joy and happiness, your own dignity, power, and beauty.

"The simple step of a courageous individual is not to take part in the lie."

~ Aleksandr Solzhenitsyn

50.   WHAT CALLS YOU

"Every human being is intended to have a character of his own;
to be what no others are, and to do what no other can do."

~ William Channing

In an attempt to suppress essential human freedom, Authoritarian regimes try to shape citizens into a faceless dull sameness, where creativity, critical analysis, and even the slightest whisper of dissent are fiercely repressed. At a much more subtle level, the same manipulation occurs in some spiritual scenes. In such cases, dogma is mistaken for direct experience and self-deception is projected as self-realization. As a result, the cult of conformity is born, and the indoctrination of a mind occurs. It makes you wonder why some people feel that it's better to 'believe and belong' than to authentically quest at one's edge.

"We can never be born enough."

~ e.e. cummings

"Belief is the death of intelligence," Robert Anton Wilson tells us. "As soon as one believes a doctrine of any sort, or assumes certitude, one stops thinking about that aspect of existence." J Krishnamurti says it this way: "I maintain that truth is a pathless land, and you cannot approach it by any path whatsoever, by any religion, by any sect. Truth, being limitless...cannot be organized; nor should any organization be formed to lead or to coerce people along any particular path. If you first understand that, then you will see how impossible it is to organize a belief. A belief is purely an individual matter, and you cannot and must not organize it. If you do, it becomes dead, crystallized; it becomes a creed, a sect, a religion, to be imposed on others."

Professor Noam Chomsky reminds us of the task at hand. "For those who stubbornly seek freedom, there can be no more urgent task than to understand the practices and mechanisms of indoctrination, which is so easy to perceive in the totalitarian societies, but much less so in the systems of 'brainwashing under freedom,' to which we are subjected, and which, all too often, we serve as willing, or unwitting instruments."

"Our mental environment is a common-property resource like the air or the water," writes Kalle Lasn, the founder of *Adbusters* magazine. "We need to protect ourselves from unwanted incursions into it, much the same way we lobbied for nonsmoking areas ten years ago."

The edge against which we test our truth is not merely that given or, in some cases, enforced by 'outside' authority. Still sharper are the edges hidden in the conformity to our own self-image, whether ideal or apathetic.

Nathaniel Hawthorne explains the burden of the divided self, this way: "No man [or woman] can wear one face to himself [or herself] and another to the multitude without finally getting bewildered as to which may be true."

Authenticity then becomes relative to what calls most deeply. The contradictions and imperfections of the present become merely apparent, not absolute. There is no standard to which we must adhere. How could there be when we create, and annihilate, all opposites with every true act of trust?

> "Integrity has no need of rules."
>
> ~ **Albert Camus**

51. BLOW ON THE FLAMES

There is no ultimate teaching to learn on the nature of being human. Consciousness is the teaching.

Existence is the guide.

As life, we are the living art of pure Beingness, exploring, and expressing love and liberation in ways that nurture our most whole sense of humanity.

There is no core philosophy that will free our minds. Being free frees the mind.

Freedom is the only religion and it's where all true religions meet.

"Caged birds sing of freedom, free birds fly."

~ Thorolf Rafto

Gandhi called freedom "...the breath of life."

Juan Goytisoloa, the Spanish poet and novelist, warns us to be watchful of shackling freedom as a fixed idea, a fixed identity, fixations of all kinds, stating: "We live in a world of rigid frontiers, often traced in blood, and of fixed, exclusive identities, and those of us who refuse to accept them are [often] the object of suspicion and allegations." And every attempt is often made to drive us away into "a no-man's land," he continues, "in which complexity is seen as anomalous and interest in difference an oddity to be stigmatized."

> "An artist is only an artist on the condition he neglects no aspect of his dual nature. This dualism is the power of being oneself and someone else one at the same time."
>
> ~ **Charles Baudelaire**

Being free includes refusing conformity and "conformity" is what John Kennedy called "the jailer of freedom and the enemy of growth." Buckminster Fuller offers us direction on deciding what each of us can do with our freedom to help transform the world, stating: "The things to do are: the things that need doing; that you see need to be done, and that no one else seems to see need to be done. Then you will conceive your own way of doing that which needs to be done — that no one else has told you to do or how to do it. This will bring out the real you that often gets buried inside a character that has acquired a superficial array of behaviors induced or imposed by others on the individual."

"The artist's imagination wards off the despair of the world," the Irish film director John Boorman writes. "Creation affords man the possibility of inventing his own future, of imagining his own world and celebrating a ritual which brings him close to the collective unconscious."

Let us remember: The global revolution will take fire not when an ideal vision is imposed on who we are, but when we *blow on the flames* of who we know we could become.

> "Sometimes, 24 hours can bring a total revolutionary change."
>
> ~ **Aung San Suu Kyi**

52.   NEVER GIVE UP

"*The* word courage comes from the same stem as the French word *Coeur*, meaning "heart," Rollo May tells us. "Thus, just as one's heart, by pumping blood to one's arms, legs, and brain enables all the other physical organs to function, so courage makes possible all the psychological virtues. Without courage other values wither away into mere facsimiles of virtue."

When I think of courage I think of my dear friend, who at age thirty was diagnosed with an inoperable, 'always terminal,' cancer. Her response was a stunning example of "grace under pressure."

After her diagnosis, her doctor compassionately discouraged her from chemotherapy, giving her just a few weeks to live. But she refused to die without a fight. Every weekend she would go to the hospital for treatment and from Monday through Wednesday she was so sick and weak she couldn't get out of bed.

Never once did she complain or lose hope.

Thursdays were the only day of the week she was strong enough to walk, before going back into the hospital on Friday for forty-eight more hours of chemotherapy. I remember every Thursday walking with her slowly along the beach in the windy chill of winter and every time she would undress and jump into the frigid ocean.

Her spontaneity and fearlessness were in themselves a magnificent teaching. My friend turned her illness into a gift for herself and those of us who were blessed to be near her.

She smiled at strangers, and even asked sometimes if they cared to stop and talk. It was her one free day a week and she used it completely. She would dance on the beach, and sometimes fall over because she was so weak. She would sing children's songs to the seagulls as we walked. She would hang out with the homeless and ask them questions about their lives. She cared more about life each week, despite her doctor's insistence that she stop hoping because there was no hope.

She didn't stop.

Eventually we did stop going to the beach on Thursdays. Instead, she went back to the hospital and comforted the women in her cancer ward who were also terminal.

She lives today, over two decades later.

The message: *Never give up.*

53.   NATURAL FREEDOM

"One's philosophy is not best expressed in words; it is expressed
in the choices one makes. In the long run, we shape our lives and
we shape ourselves."

~ **Eleanor Roosevelt**

*H*uman authenticity should not be mistaken for a homogeneous imagination where one style fits all.

There is no *look* that one should adopt.

We are divine beings, not entities to program into mere functions, or manufacture as mannequins to serve the needs of an elite.

Slavery, forced or self-induced, is wrong.

What value is there in adapting to confinement?

"All I can do is be me, whoever that is."

~ **Bob Dylan**

Finding our liberation through living involves a deep personal trust in the inherent rightness of our humanness; our natural freedom. We are not concerned with angling toward or away from any one state or the other, whether it is silence or sound, movement or stillness, being or doing, freedom or bondage, the personal or the transpersonal.

Natural freedom embraces everything and consciously stops attempting to synchronize with perfection. The most perfect people inevitably have the narrowest outlooks. Self-images are like that. Even the most transparent are suits of armor. Like cellophane, you can see through them, but unless you unwrap from them you can't get out.

"Each time we affirm one part of us, we deny another.'

~ Octivo Paz

54.   I AM ME

"The hallmark of courage in our age of conformity is the capacity to stand on one's convictions, not obstinately or defiantly (these are gestures of defensiveness, not courage) nor as a gesture of retaliation, but simply because these are what one believes."

~ Rollo May

*A*uthenticity arises naturally out of an abiding respect for our ability to live and die right now with a shameless sense of wholeness and self-respect.

"I am me," states Virginia Satir. "In all the world, there is no one else exactly like me. ... I own everything about me: my body, my feelings, my mouth, my voice, all my actions, whether they be to others or myself. I own my fantasies, my dreams, my hopes, my fears. I own my triumphs and successes, all my failures and mistakes. Because I own all of me, I can become intimately acquainted... and be friendly with all my parts."

"I must be myself," Emerson once declared. "If you can love me for what I am, we shall be happier. If you cannot, I will still seek to deserve that you should. I will not hide my tastes or aversions. I will...trust...what is deep is holy."

Sometimes I stop and ask myself how deeply I feel my innate divinity. How dependent am I on other people's mental life?

"Whenever we pursue noble goals, obstacles and difficulties are bound to occur. As human beings, we may lose hope. But there is nothing to be gained from discouragement; our determination must be very firm. According to my meager experience, we can change. We can transform ourselves."

~ 14th Dalai Lama

55. TOWARD THE INACCESSIBLE

"Courage is the foundation of integrity."

~ **Keshavan Nair**

In your quest for freedom bring an unrelenting honesty that respects truth more than your opinions about it. As falsity is seen, realign to reality. This process of self-accountability often forces one to become undone, releasing us from limiting thoughts and behaviors — to create and explore, to transform this life we are just waking up to.

As self-respect strengthens, fear subsides, and understanding matures, we come to appreciate that even mistakes, even breakdowns, are preferable to artificial behaviors. We know the importance of imagination, of creativity. We know the importance of openness — not settling on conclusions about truth and transformation. This requires a trust in the inherent sanctity of our being. There are so many ways to enhance the dance — ways to stretch, open, and create. Picasso said, "It took me my entire life to learn how to paint like a child."

What does it mean to re-enchant our innocence? What does it mean to disengage from self-defeating patterns of pseudo-safety? How do we break the trance of religion-fuelled dogma, jump off the wheel of blind consumerism, or reel in our reckless rebel and re-inspire the urge for existential adventure?

"Deep down, all of us are probably aware that some kind of mystical evolution is our true task," Tom Robbins writes. "Yet we suppress the notion with considerable force because to admit it is to admit that most of our political gyrations, religious dogmas, social ambitions, and financial ploys are not merely counter-productive but trivial."

"Not everything assumes a name. Some things lead beyond words. Art inflames even a frozen, darkened soul to a high spiritual experience," Aleksandr Solzhenitsyn tells us. "Through Art we are sometimes visited — dimly, briefly — by revelations such as cannot be produced by rational thinking. Like that little looking-glass from the fairy-tales: look into it and you will see...the Inaccessible."

What do you see?

56.   BEDAZZLED

"A human being is a spirit. But what is spirit? Spirit is the self. But what is the self? The self is a relation that relates itself to itself or is the relation relating itself to itself in the relation."

~ Søren Kierkegaard

*A*s we know, nothing stands alone.
Nothing stays the same.
Everything is conditioned and interdependent.
Every perception is in flux.

Our faces.
Our hearts.
Our memory.
Life is a sand castle constantly eroded by limitless time. Awareness itself, and for that matter stillness too, are not static states.

Nothing is — everything changes.
Every condition is a condition.

Consciousness and its contents are an
ephemeral house of cards.

Awareness can also look upon consciousness and dissolve itself therein, like a wave merging back into the sea, or a rainbow disappearing in the sky. Awareness can also occupy this playland of heightened-mind — morphing by virtue of a will that seems indivisible from life itself.

Consciousness can also feel infinite, or invisible.
Or anything in between.

The Tibetan Buddhist teacher, Nyoshul Khenpo, in speaking about the mind's true nature, states: "After his great awakening...Buddha said that the ultimate nature of mind [was] perfectly pure, profound, quiescent, luminous, uncompounded, unconditioned, unborn and undying, and free since the beginningless beginning. When we examine this mind for ourselves it becomes apparent that its inherent openness, clarity, and cognizant quality comprise what is known as innate wakefulness, primordial nondual Awareness: *rigpa*.

"This is our birthright, our true nature," he goes onto say.
"It is not something missing, to be sought and obtained.
It is the very heart of our original existential being."

How seductive it is to abide here, to become bedazzled with the physics of consciousness, this singular state of "primordial nondual awareness."

Could it be that the only way to make sense
out of change, is to do as
Alan Watts suggested?

Just "plunge into it,
move with it, and join the Dance."

And we must ask,
is there an Absolute Enlightened
way to dance with change?

57. YOUR OWN MINDSCAPE

Becoming alive to the imperfect present is a pointing to a liberating way of being, dynamically free — a love of adventure, experimentation, radical presence.

The awakening of a *whole world dharma* is not a doctrine that can be memorized and followed step by step.

There's no schema that can be followed
that guarantees freedom.

When in doubt, reflect: there is no 'single right way' to Be.
There is no right way to delight in spontaneity.
There is no right way to believe in ourselves.

Or to risk curiosity, or to wonder, or to Be so alive and open and original that we learn "to love things as no one has thought to love them," as the poet Rainer Maria Rilke suggested.

"Draw this line, only as you feel it to be the most worthwhile act of your life."

~ Paul Reps

We are in a universe of infinite possibilities,
framed by mortality, imagination, mystery.

"The biggest challenge in jazz improvisation," Miles Davis observed, "is not to play all the notes you could play, but to wait, hesitate — to play what's not there."

"The basic step in achieving inward freedom is 'choosing one's self,'" Rollo May informs us. "[This] means 'to affirm one's responsibility for one's self and one's existence.' It is the attitude which is opposite to blind momentum or routine existence; it is an attitude of aliveness or decisiveness; it means that one recognizes that he [and she] exists in his particular spot in the universe, and he accepts the responsibility for his existence, responsibility for fulfilling one's destiny, accepting the fact that one must make his choices himself."

"If someone is guiding you, that is suspicious, because you are relying on something external," Chögyam Trungpa once said. "Being fully what you are in yourself becomes guidance."

What does it mean to become fully what you are in yourself?

"Wisdom tells me I am nothing. Love tells me I am everything. And between the two my life flows."

~ Sri Nisargadatta Maharaj

Be alive.
Use your freedom.
Create your own unique mindscape.

58.   IN OUR MINDS

"[The] scientific exploration of human consciousness is just an extension of the arts, theater, literature, and even religion. We are returning to a project that has moved human beings for centuries: to apply the mind to its own understanding."

~ **Bernard Baars**

*T*he awakening of consciousness is saying that from the very depth of our being there is a natural, creative intelligence that holds the answers to existence.

"The more deeply I search for the roots of our global environmental crisis," states Al Gore, "the more I am convinced that it is an outer manifestation of an inner crisis that is, for lack of a better word, spiritual."

I firmly believe that by taming the afflictive forces within consciousness, we have the best chances of survival, while ending our degradation of the planet.

Vaclav Havel, the former president of the Czech Republic, stated in an address to the United States Congress that "Without a global revolution in the sphere of human consciousness, nothing will change for the better. And the catastrophe toward which this world is headed — ecological, social and demographic — will be unavoidable."

I think we are aware at this point that we must all wake up, individually and collectively, to how our inner world impacts the outer world.

Consciousness is our bond with all life.

It is our common heritage.
It is our wilderness.
Our paradise.
Our prison.
Our bliss.

> We inhabit the 'known' as if on an island while the
> great unknown remains like a mountain submerged
> infinitely deep within the ocean of the unconscious.

> When and why things emerge from its inner
> depths remains largely a mystery.

What we do know is that the mind can be what we make it.

It can be friend or foe.
It can give life or take it.

It can serve or enslave.
It can give hope or destroy it.

It can dream or denigrate.
It can create beauty or concoct evil.

It's all right there behind our eyes,
in and around us too.

And its exploration and development
has never been more important.

As the 14th Dalai Lama so famously said, "Perhaps now that
the Western sciences have reached down into the atom and

out into the cosmos finally to realize the extreme vulnerability of all life and its value, it is becoming obvious that the field of what we call 'inner science' — dealing with inner things — is of supreme importance."

"Here is my advice as we begin the century," Gerard K. O'Neill writes. "First, guard the freedom of ideas at all costs. Be alert that dictators have always played on the natural human tendency to blame others and to oversimplify. And don't regard yourself as a guardian of freedom unless you respect and preserve the rights of people you disagree with to free, public, unhampered expression."

"Just as wars begin in the minds of men, peace also begins in our minds. The same species who invented war is capable of inventing peace."

~ UNESCO Charter

59. PROPHET OF THE PAST

"For thousands of generations people lived and reproduced with no need to know how the machinery of the brain works. Myth and self-deception, tribal identity and ritual, more than objective truth, gave them the adaptive edge."

~ Edward O Wilson

*T*o explorethe interface of mind with life as source for both personal and planetary transformation one must be vigilant in bringing the highest standards of empirical inquiry to bear upon the process of perception.

Nietzsche defined freedom as "the will to be responsible to ourselves." This to me means the ability to respond to our instinct for freedom. Ability here means competence and skill. In other words, wise discernment and intellectual rigor play vital roles as we open to the contents of consciousness and examine the role of perception as the architecture of reality.

"Most people think that shadows follow, precede or surround beings or objects. The truth is that they also surround words, ideas, desires, deeds, impulses and memories."

~ Elie Wiesel

William Sumner, the American sociologist, in explaining the meaning and importance of critical thinking, states: "It is the examination and test of propositions of any kind which are offered for acceptance, in order to find out whether they correspond to reality or not. The critical faculty is a product of education and training. It is a mental habit and power. It is a prime condition of human welfare that men and women should be trained in it." He concludes by saying, "It is our only guarantee against delusion, deception, superstition, and misapprehension of ourselves and our earthly circumstances."

What is dogma?

"Dogma is the established belief or doctrine held by a religion, ideology or any kind of organization: it is authoritative and not to be disputed, doubted or diverged from. At the core of the dogma concept is Absolutism, infallibility, irrefutability, unquestioned acceptance (among adherents) and anti-skepticism."

~ Wikipedia

George Steiner, philosopher and prolific author on the impact of the Holocaust, made the stark observation: "We know now that a man can read Goethe or Rilke in the evening, that he can play Bach and Schubert, and go to his day's work at Auschwitz in the morning."

How is such a corruption of conscience possible?

Ernest Becker, in his book *The Denial of Death* offers an explanation, stating: "If we had to offer the briefest explanation of all the evil men have wreaked upon themselves and upon their world since the beginning of time, it would be simply in the toll that his *pretense to sanity* takes as he tries to deny his true condition."

May his words serve as an eternal reminder of the mind's maddening capacity for self-deception and the urgent need for developing our faculty for critical discernment.

"The act of looking backward is, just like that of looking into the future, an act of divination," stated Kierkegaard. "And if the prophet is well called an historian of the future, the historian is just as well called, or even better so, a prophet of the past, of the historical."

> "We have to face the fact that either all of us are going to die together, or we are going to learn to live together, and to do that we have to learn how to talk with each other."
>
> ~ **Eleanor Roosevelt**

"Suppose we were able to share meanings freely," the physicist David Bohm asks, "without a compulsive urge to impose our view or conform to those of others and without distortion and self-deception. Would this not constitute a real revolution in culture?"

> "I am determined to practice deep listening.
> I am determined to practice loving speech."
>
> ~ **Thich Nhat Hanh**

60. THE MATRIX WITHIN

Among the great mysteries of the world, such as the origins of life, space, time, and gravity, the mystery of consciousness is perhaps the least understood. The only thing we know with certainty is that this virtual world of complex energies, sheathed in flesh, exists.

Consciousness is as central to life as the ecosystem is to the earth.

We can't live without it, nor can it be escaped.

Consciousness is home.

Alan Watts said it this way: "We must see that consciousness is neither an isolated soul nor the mere function of a single nervous system, but of that totality of interrelated stars and galaxies which makes a nervous system possible."

From consciousness our world comes into being.

It is where we form identities, create myths, and fabricate illusions.

It is where values are forged, principles are shaped, and freedom is known.

By realizing that consciousness is *the matrix within* which all that we think, feel, and know is born, an impassioned self-responsibility arises.

"We are slaves to what we do not know; of what we know we are masters," states Sri Nisargadatta Maharaj, the Indian spiritual teacher. "Whatever vice or weakness in ourselves, if we discover and understand its causes and its workings, we overcome it by the very knowing."

In other words, neglect consciousness — denigrate it, violate it — and, like the earth, the individual suffers, and often causes suffering too.

On the other hand, nurture consciousness — understand its nature, inhabit it wisely — and we flourish, and elevate society too.

"I suppose one seeks greatness through taming one's passions," Aung San Suu Kyi once told me. "And isn't there a saying that 'it is far more difficult to conquer yourself than to conquer the rest of the world'? So, I think the taming of one's own passions, in the Buddhist way of thinking, is the chief way to greatness, no matter what the circumstances may be. For example, a lot of our supporters meditate when they're in prison...because it's a very sensible thing to do. That is to say do what you can with the world inside you in order to bring it under proper control."

"Hatred can rot away at a person's intelligence and conscience. Enemy mentality will poison the spirit of a nation, incite cruel mortal struggles, destroy a society's tolerance and humanity, and hinder a nation's progress toward freedom and democracy. That is why I hope to be able to transcend my personal experiences as I look upon our nation's development and social change, to counter the regime's hostility with utmost goodwill, and to dispel hatred with love."

~ Liu Xiao, imprisoned Nobel Peace Prize Winner 2010, *I Have No Enemies*

61.   MINDFUL INTERACTION

"The history of the world is none other than the progress of the
consciousness of freedom."

~ G. W. F. Hegel

Consciousness is a holographic-like excitation of cognitive
properties. It has no center and no singular reality that is the
inherent reference point for subjective experience. In other
words, consciousness is a coreless circuitry of comprehensible
functionings. Whereas, awareness, or mindfulness, is the
quality of mind that functions to directly experience the
contents of consciousness prior to intellectual reflection and
philosophical speculation.

To embody awareness as a 'way of life' requires learning the
art of *mindful interaction,* while re-enchanting 'the wisdom of
no escape.'

In other words, how could there be any other place to 'be'
than where we are?

From this lived vantage point, a wellspring of hope arises —
the gratitude that you've arrived at the convergence of where
life authentically meets itself, right here, right now.

As Kalu Rinpoche so famously said, "We live in illusion
and the appearance of things. There is a reality. *We are that
reality.* When you understand this, you see that you are
nothing, and being nothing, you are everything. That is all."

The depth of this realization proportionately interrupts the twin habits of projecting illusions and clamoring over the past. As this insight is assimilated, a cognitive symmetry arises where the inner and outer merge into a unified wholeness, while mindfulness itself becomes a transformational power — harmonizing consciousness, evolving its lucidity, sensitivity, and luminosity.

> Mindfulness also relaxes mental posturing and relieves the contraction of personas, revealing a much more nuanced experience of pure being.

As awareness matures further, it begins to arise effortlessly. It is here that consciousness begins to discover the substructures of its own functioning.

From an understanding of *impermanence* the mind progressively releases clinging.

From an understanding of *suchness* the mind dissolves ignorance, the belief in a subjective, unchanging self.

From an understanding of *conditioned arising* consciousness honors its natural state, a transparent wisdom that knows but does not grasp.

> "As the great ocean has but one taste — the taste of salt —" the Buddha declared. "The *dharma* has but one taste — the taste of freedom."

62. FULL AND EMPTY

"We are at war between consciousness and nature,"
Alan Watts writes, "between the desire for permanence
and the fact of flux. It is our self against ourselves."

*M*indfulness by function divests the mind of its insidious
tendency to fuse, grasp or cling to perceptions — emotions,
images, and ideas — as personal or permanent; identifying
them as 'my' experience, 'my' feelings, 'my' understanding,
and so on. This unquestioned habit to selectively fixate on
objects of perception reveals that in the absence of fixation
there is also the absence of conflict.

"Because we cannot accept the truth of transience, we suffer,"
states Suzuki Roshi.

"People have a hard time letting go of their suffering,"
Thich Nhat Hanh explains. "Out of a fear of the
unknown, they prefer suffering that is familiar."

As inner dissonance ceases, the mind becomes unified, at
ease within its own movement, and the oscillation toward or
away from anything no longer holds appeal.

One simply sees 'things' as they arise while participating in
the experience freely — without fear or fixation.

Here there is no faith required, other than a trust in that
which your awareness reveals about your own being.

There is no god to believe in, no cosmic deities to honor, and no gurus to worship.

Nothing to accept nor reject.

Life is what it is — nothing more, nothing less, full and empty at the same time.

"Let the self-contraction relax into the empty ground of its own awareness, and let it there quietly die," Ken Wilber states. "See the Kosmos arise in its place, dancing madly and divine, self-luminous and self-liberating...transparent images shimmering in the radiant Abyss."

Nyoshul Khen Rinpoche described the nature of Awakened consciousness as, "Profound and tranquil, free from complexity, uncompounded luminous clarity, beyond the mind of conceptual ideas. In this there is not a thing to be removed, nor anything that needs to be added. It is merely the immaculate looking naturally at itself."

Non sine sole iris

No rainbow without the sun.

63. COGNITIVE EVOLUTION

There is no Mecca outside the Mystery itself. How can one attain anything lasting in an unstable and passing world? Is there anything that isn't propped up by conditions? Isn't the universe an immeasurably complex field of interlocking waves and particles where nothing exists apart from everything else?

> Is there anything that exists outside or inside of our interrelated infinity? Let us acknowledge the essential mystery of it all, and go from there.

But the mystery is not just 'out there.' It's internal too. The brain, for instance, this 3 pound organ with its 100 billion neurons that have a cognitive functioning capacity of about 75 years, remains largely a mystery. And the idea that the finite brain can comprehend the infinite structures of an infinite cosmos, with incalculable realities, embraced by limitless time is, of course, mindless.

> "Freedom is a mystery," Octavio Paz states. "Freedom depends on the very thing that limits or denies it — fate, God, biological or social determinism, whatever...
> — *a freedom that is always precarious."*

"But then, neither do we know how or even if it is the brain that 'knows,'" states Martin Kovan. "It may be that the brain is still a resilient but limited form (of hardware) with regard to the potentially limitless evolution of the mind (as software). And that cognitive evolution, as we have seen, has barely begun in terms of cosmological time. It seems safe to say that what we don't know now, the species may very well take as self-evident some millennia down the track."

> "It requires a very unusual mind to undertake the analysis of the obvious," Alfred North Whitehead once quipped. That is to say: Transcendent perfection is beyond our grasp at this time in human history.

Let us remember: To aspire to or dream of 'perfection' is one thing. But there is a catch: we are human, and that humanity IS precisely what makes this life so worthwhile.

Alfred North Whitehead concludes with his encouraging words: "Our minds are finite, and yet even in these circumstances of finitude we are surrounded by possibilities that are infinite, and the purpose of life is to grasp as much as we can out of that Infinitude."

64. WHOLENESS DANCING

"The life of God — the life which the mind apprehends and enjoys as
it rises to the absolute unity of all things — may be described as a
play of love with itself."

~ **G.W.F. Hegel**

Freedom is not the emancipation of consciousness from all
forms of conflict.

Nor is it the absolute end of human suffering.

We are free when attuned
to the rhythm of our own uniqueness,
listening to the wisdom of our own hearts.

This requires a radical acceptance of
who we are and feel ourselves to be.

Martha Graham, the legendary dancer, said,
"The center of the stage is where I am."

Make where you are in your heart, center stage.
In other words, let nothing take primacy over presence.

"I did not want to be a tree, a flower or a wave," she continues.
"In a dancer's body, we as audience must see ourselves,
not the imitated behavior of everyday actions, not the
phenomenon of nature, not exotic creatures from another
planet, but something of a miracle." The miracle of 'you' —
the full expression of your essential being, your free flowing

sense of wholeness, dancing — "the play of love" — with the people dearest to you in your life. And from there, expanding outward, if you so choose.

"There is no instinct like that of the heart."

~ **Lord Byron**

65. CONSCIOUS CHOICE

It's not through exploring our inner depths
alone that we relate to others.

*T*o *open our eyes*, to turn outward and witness suffering we must engage in humankind's quintessential struggle: we find ourselves — mortal, fragile, imperfect — inside a world fraught with staggering expressions of ignorance.

This conundrum is the central equation our existence must face.

Clearly, our shared struggle for freedom and planetary survival is a complex tapestry of interwoven impulses, images, feelings, actions, and decisions — a life-long experience containing every conceivable paradox, outrage, and injustice.

Equally as clear, is that there is no foolproof resolution to the phenomenon of being alive. Insights come slowly. Progress depends on you and me.

Definitions of the word paradigm vary but it basically means: 'A constellation of concepts, values, perceptions and practices held by an individual or shared by a community or a country which forms a particular vision of reality that is the basis of the way an individual, community, group, or country organizes itself.' Webster's Dictionary defines it as: A set of assumptions, concepts, values, and practices that constitutes a way of viewing reality for the community that shares them; a philosophical or theoretical framework of any kind.

Simply stated, each of us has our own set of paradigms or lenses through which we view each other and the world. These perception-filters determining the "way we see things" may potentially obscure our ability to consider new or different frameworks of thinking, especially if they conflict with our pre-existing perceptions of what truth or reality is.

In 1962, the physicist, Thomas Kuhn, developed the concept of a "paradigm shift." On the other hand, people who are 'inwardly stuck' or unable to make an 'inner shift' can be said to be suffering from "paradigm paralysis", or the inability or refusal to see beyond their current models of thinking, or the impact they have on others and the world.

Dr. Helen Caldicott, co-founder of Physicians for Social Responsibility and author of *The New Nuclear Danger*, was asked, "What actions can we as responsible citizens take in the face of the new nuclear danger? What can we say to people who are in denial of the problem?"

Dr. Caldicott answered, "This is the ultimate spiritual and religious issue ever to face the human race. For what is our responsibility to preserve creation and evolution? We are the curators of possibly the only life in the universe and our responsibility is enormous. We must therefore dedicate every moment to the preservation of creation. But first, action must be preceded by education. We are all physicians to a planet that is in the intensive care unit. *The New Nuclear Danger* is now the *Grays Anatomy* for a new breed of global physicians. Learn it and you will become ultimately powerful and equipped with the necessary knowledge that will drive our new crusade for global preservation."

Essentially, what Dr. Caldicott is saying is that the survival of life as we know it, depends on an urgent mass paradigm shift. In other words, we must learn to live more fully through conscious choice rather than through paradigms of unconscious programming.

How to increase our ability to make conscious choices?

Ken Keyes, Jr. suggests 'practicing freedom' in this way: exercise "observing consciousness" — the employment of mindful self-awareness. Whenever you feel unable to be the person you want to be, Keyes suggests, "Observe yourself: 1). Observe your emotions; what am I feeling? 2). Observe your thoughts; what are the judgements, attitudes or perspectives I have that are causing these emotions? 3). Look at your options: a) change the situation. b) change your thinking about the situation. c) leave the situation. d) or stay stuck."

In other words, he concludes, "To see your [ignorance] clearly is to be liberated from it." And like all other talents, liberation requires training, through relationships, to self, others, earth, cosmos, conflicts and peace; everything.

"Freedom is nothing else but a chance to be better."

~ **Albert Camus**

66.   A LARGER STORY

Transforming ignorance requires persistent awareness and honesty. It takes courage to resist the impulse to hide in axiomatic truths, philosophical or religious dogmas, or so-called spiritual realizations with their promises of access to realms of "perfect-inner-beingness." Although I firmly believe in the need to evolve our understanding of human consciousness to better serve civilization and to peacefully explore outer space, I do not believe in Absolute answers.

"It's only the shallow who know themselves, "Oscar Wilde once quipped. I find his witticism — directed to those who had imprisoned him for exposing their homophobia and sexual hypocrisy — not only wise and liberating but illuminating as well. His words point to the ego's tendency to become bloated on its own self-importance. They also invite us into humility by reflecting on life's mystery and inexhaustible subtlety.

"The quest for certainty blocks the search for meaning," Erich Fromm writes. "Uncertainty is the very condition to impel man [and woman] to unfold his [and her] powers."

Although as mortals we are constantly struggling towards truth, and never in full possession of it, be brave: Think Beyond your time.

"If you doubt that asking a new question is a royal road to revolution, transformation, and renewal," states Sam Keen, "consider what happened when Descartes asked, "Of what may I be certain?" or when Newton asked, "How is a falling apple like a rising moon?" or when Marx asked, "Why were men born free but are everywhere in chains?" Your question is the quest you're on. No questions — no journey. Timid questions — timid trips. Radical questions — an expedition to the root of your being."

"It is change, continuing change, inevitable change," Isaac Asimov tells us, "that is the dominant factor in society today. No sensible decision can be made any longer without taking into account not only the world as it is, but the world as it will be."

The following is the last paragraph of Andrei
Sakharov's Nobel Lecture when awarded
the Peace Prize on December 11, 1975.

"Thousands of years ago, tribes of human beings suffered great privations in the struggle to survive. In this struggle it was important not only to be able to handle a club, but also to possess the ability to think reasonably, to take care of the knowledge and experience garnered by the tribe, and to develop the links that would provide cooperation with other tribes. Today the entire human race is faced with a similar test. In infinite space many civilizations are bound to exist, among them civilizations that are also wiser and more "successful" than ours. I support the cosmological hypothesis which states that the development of the universe is repeated in its basic features an infinite number of times. In accordance with this, other civilizations, including more "successful" ones, should exist an infinite number of times on the "preceding" and the "following" pages of the Book of the Universe. Yet this should not minimize our sacred endeavors in this world of ours, where, like faint glimmers of light in the dark, we have emerged for a moment from the nothingness of dark unconsciousness of material existence. We must make good the demands of reason and create a life worthy of ourselves and of the goals we only dimly perceive."

Jean Houston, in speaking about visionary transformation, explains that we must "die to one story, one myth, in order to be reborn to a larger one. This involves giving up a smaller story in order to wake up to a larger story."

What is the larger story you are waking up to?

67.   TOTAL RESPONSIBILITY

> "You actually cannot sell the idea of freedom, democracy, diversity, as
> if it were a brand attribute and not reality — not at the same time as
> you're bombing people, you can't."
>
> ~ **Naomi Klein**

"I am superior to you only in one point," Narcissus tells Goldmund in Hermann Hesse's novel *Narcissus and Goldmund.* "I'm awake, whereas you are only half awake, or completely asleep sometimes. I call a man awake who knows in his conscious reason his innermost unreasonable forces, drives, and weaknesses, and knows how to deal with them."

As humans we are bound by conditions not of our own making. By virtue of birth, complexity and confusion cannot be avoided. They are conditions inborn to every person. In other words, ignorance is innate to the operating system. Ignorance means partial clarity or, in some cases, blindness to reality. With ignorance, errors in discretion are inevitable. If ignorance arises with other states of mind, such as anger or judgements, one often creates an imagined reality and then projects blame on it, thus scapegoating a phantom that doesn't actually exist, certainly not in the way that one's blame suggests it does.

In this way, ignorance is a type of mental hallucination that functions to allow humans to castigate life with their primordial delusions, those biases, prejudices, and a host of other emotional and psychological distortions that started long before the 'circumstances' deprived you of 'your happiness.'

"Take care your worship, those things over there are not giants, but windmills."
~ **Miguel de Cervantes (1605)**

"Analysis as an instrument of civilization is good," Thomas Mann states, "in so far as it shatters absurd convictions, acts as a solvent upon natural prejudices, and undermines authority; Good, in other words, in that it sets free, refines, humanizes, makes slaves ripe for freedom."

Of course, the notion of mental projection is easy to understand, but in the heat of the moment, where passions and attachments run deep, it is a challenging obstacle to overcome, requiring nothing less than total responsibility for the self-generated state of one's own mind.

Edwin Markham, the American poet, writes: "He drew a circle to shut me out — Heretic, rebel, a thing to flout. But
Love and I had the wit to win;
We drew a circle that took him in."

68. THE BRIDGE IS LOVE

A compassionate response to suffering understands our human drive for escape. But to resist the desire to escape, to embrace the many dimensions of our humanness, requires the courage to feel many unpleasant things.

"The Burmese expression for refugee is *dukkha-the*, 'one who has to bear *dukkha*, or suffering,'" Aung San Suu Kyi tells us. "In that sense, none of us can avoid knowing what it is to be a refugee."

We live with the anxiety of an unpredictable world where the unthinkable often happens. Samantha Power, the Pulitzer Prize-winning author, speaks to the unthinkable with stark clarity, stating: "There is a difference between knowledge of facts and deep, visceral knowledge — the kind...that makes you cry, the kind that makes you — if only for an instant — imagine your daughter being forced into round-the-clock service in a Serbian rape camp, or your little boy being reduced to pleading to a machete-wielding Rwandan extremist, 'Please don't kill me. I'll never be Tutsi again.'"

Yet no matter how dark it gets can self-transformation really be found? Can beauty be found in the most terrible circumstances?

Susan Griffin, the eco-feminist author shares how she feels the transformation takes place: "Simply to speak the truth heals. The blood of the wound heals the wound. To speak to a receiving ear, to be understood, even if only by one another, or by oneself heals. And for every part of ourselves that we hide in darkness, for every lie that we tell ourselves, we suffer. Separated from our authentic cries, we become weak imitations of who it is we think we should be. We build our lives after a diminished image of humanness. And this diminishment is part of any image, no matter how humane, that does not treasure darkness."

> "There is a land of the living and a land of the dead and the bridge is love, the only survival, the only meaning."
>
> ~ **Thornton Wilder**

69.   ONE'S OWN WAY

Life is a moment-to-moment process of decisions and the thin line between them — between the life we are leading and the life we could be leading — is often a hair's-breadth in difference.

Yet freedom is always there.

We are free the moment we choose to be.

Choice is always there.

Every second can be a choice to exercise freedom.

The freedom to think.

The freedom to speak.

The freedom to act.

What we do with our freedom will change, but the more we release the energy of freedom from the constraints of conditions, the more liberated we become.

Victor Frankel, the Viennese psychiatrist, made this observation from his years in Auschwitz: "We who lived in concentration camps can remember those who walked through the huts comforting others, giving away their last piece of bread. They may have been few in number, but they offer sufficient proof that everything can be taken from a person but one thing: the last of human freedoms — to choose one's attitude in any given set of circumstances — to choose one's own way."

"Few will have the greatness to bend history itself," Robert Kennedy once said. "But each of us can work to change a small portion of events, and in the total of all those acts will be written the history of this generation."

> "The most common way people give up their power is by thinking they don't have any."
>
> ~ **Alice Walker**

70.   MASTER YOUR MIND

"As far as we can discern," Carl Jung states, "the sole purpose of human existence is to kindle a light of meaning in the darkness of mere being."

*T*o be true to oneself is a radical act of bravery. Because, as it builds in power, it subverts the mechanisms of conformity and compromise. It confronts the status quo of our own fear, and whatever external circumstances onto which we project that fear.

The South African anti-apartheid activist, Steven Biko, clubbed to death by government security forces, made the statement: "The most potent weapon of the oppressor is the mind of the oppressed." In other words, *to know yourself* is to be invulnerable to the mind of the aggressor.

To own your mind is a powerful force.

"If you love yourself, then you don't give your power away to people who hate you and want to annihilate you....that's what healing is about: finding that person buried inside us who can stand up to oppressive authority."

~ Sapphire

In Burma, Aung San Suu Kyi relentlessly encourages her fellow freedom fighters to "Feel always free. Nobody can detain [your] mind though they can detain your body... *Master your mind* and nobody can abuse you. We need to remember this."

Also in Burma, when I asked U Kyi Maung, my eighty-six year old friend and mentor who spent eleven years in solitary confinement, "what was the 'central wisdom' he lived by in prison," he replied without the slightest hesitation: "As a prisoner of conscience my freedom was not my captors to take."

71. WILLINGNESS TO FEEL

To embrace the challenge of liberation — transforming the afflictive emotions of greed, anger, and ignorance into generosity, wisdom, and love — requires a brave heart devoted to engaging every encounter, come what may, as valuable to the evolution of the whole of one's being.

Finding the wisdom of our own unique *world dharma* and evolving its power is perhaps the best contribution we can make to the future of life and freedom.

Could there be anything more important than participating in the evolution of consciousness and the future of life?

Many people speak of being 'at the edge' today, but what is it really?

"'The edge' is an expression from chaos theory...which describes the unpredictable behavior of things like the human heartbeat, beehives and the stock market," explains Danah Zohar, the MIT trained physicist. "The edge is the meeting point between order and chaos, between the known and the unknown. ... It is where new information is created."

Aware of the arising as it arises, making known the unknown, is the embodied matrix, the indispensable condition, for wisdom and freedom. These words, taken together, illuminate the basic meaning of *sanvega* — a Buddhist concept. Essentially, *sanvega* is a dynamic aliveness that courageously engages both the edge and the whole of the imperfect present.

It arouses *dharma* purpose and is manifested as immediacy and circumspection. Although it arises in the present, it draws its wisdom from the past, and propels visionary, futuristic thinking.

As *sanvega* evolves, it invokes a much more nuanced experience of *interbeing* with self, other, and world. And when developed it becomes an inextinguishable fire that fuels the actualization of one's highest life purpose, by igniting innovative acts of conscience grounded in creativity, compassion, and love.

Donald W. Shriver, Jr., President Emeritus of Union Theological Seminary, offers a sobering reminder of the value of *sanvega* as the motivation to participate more actively in the global revolution of the spirit, stating: "The agents of atrocities have a self-interest in keeping their acts invisible, buried, and publicly forgotten. The Nazis meant to plough under every death camp...In South African torture cells, the torturers taunted their victims with the prediction that, just as no one could hear their present screams, no one would remember them in the future either. The moral damages of amnesia are multiple: to victims, whose final indignity in survival or in death is to have their suffering forgotten; to perpetrators, whose moral health cannot be restored without confrontation of their immorality; and — not least — to a public that has every prudent self-interest in knowing enough about an evil past to be put on alert against its repetition."

> At the heart of *sanvega* is compassion — *a relentless willingness to feel* and to keep feeling that everybody belongs to a larger sphere of existence: life.

Sanvega also keeps encouraging us to act with well-considered dignity; to challenge our comfort zones; and to keep ourselves attuned against repetition of a misguided past, making the world a more sane and safe place, each and every day.

"The past reflects eternally between two mirrors — the bright mirror of words and deeds, and the dark one, full of things we didn't do or say."

~ **Gregory David Roberts**

72.   MYTHIC UNITY

The art and activism of freedom is a liberating process guided by the awareness that life and death are always separated by a breath. From such an awakened state of mind a new type of consciousness emerges; a rebirth as real as waking from a dream. The senses expand, momentarily cleansed of obscurations. Perceptions are enhanced, revealing much greater distinction and dimension. Sounds are accentuated. Colors become brighter. Tastes, more subtle. Smells, more fragrant. Patterns of interrelated space are felt more intimately and understood with greater clarity. Insights translate seamlessly into behavioral changes.

It is easy to fall in love with the timeless flow of just being human. It's a sublime, somewhat surreal, appreciation of just how out of this world life is.

And it simplifies us too.

There's no hurry to get somewhere.
No special state to attain or avoid.

No persona to uphold. No one to please.
Nothing to fear.

"Regard this world as a star at dawn, a bubble in a stream, a flash of lightning in a summer cloud, a flickering lamp, a phantom and a dream."

~ The Buddha

We accept our existence as dream creatures dancing on a canvas of photons. I accept you. I love you. All of you, with your weaknesses, strengths, fears, and the great unknown.

"In every crescendo of sensation, in every effort to recall, in every progress towards satisfaction of desire," said William James, "this succession of an emptiness and fullness that have reference to each other and are one flesh is the essence of the phenomenon."

Albert Einstein shared his experience of the emptiness and fullness of pure being in this way: "There are moments when one feels free from one's own identification with human limitations and inadequacies. At such moments...one stands gazing in amazement at the profoundly moving beauty of the eternal, the unfathomable: life and death flow into one, and there is neither evolution nor destiny; only Being."

Let's call this the 'unified mind' — a mind intimately at ease within its own nature, both at rest in its flawed humanness and existentially awake to its innate perfection.

"The revolution of the word is the revolution of the world," Eliot Weinberger said, "and both cannot exist without the revolution of the body: Life as Art, a return to the mythic lost unity of thought and body, man [and woman] and nature, I and other."

"I have nothing to say, I am saying it, and that is poetry."

~ **John Cage**

73.   FREEDOM-IN-ACTION

"Most humans have an almost infinite capacity for taking things for granted."

~ **Aldous Huxley**

*T*o practice the art of freedom requires the resolve to take risks and expand into new areas of being. "In a world of universal deceit, telling the truth is a revolutionary act," George Orwell famously declared. He was a cultural outlaw who refused to be embedded in the concrete of conformity.

> Salman Rushdie tells us, "A poet's work is to name the unnameable, to point at frauds, to take sides, start arguments, shape the world, and stop it going to sleep."

By being true to her conscience, Rosa Parks snapped a lot of white people out of the trance of racial prejudice. The prodemocracy demonstrators in Tiananmen Square who courageously confronted the coma of authoritarian communism were heroes and heroines of freedom. As were those in Tibet and Burma and Syria, gunned down for marching for the human right to be free, grounded in equality, dignity, and peace.

We have many exceptional examples of *freedom-in-action.*

Aung San Suu Kyi points us to the meaning of everyday revolution, daily acts that serve the greater good: "Within a system which denies the existence of basic human rights, fear tends to be the order of the day," she states. "Fear of imprisonment, fear of torture, fear of death, fear of losing friends, family, property or means of livelihood, fear of poverty, fear of isolation, fear of failure. The most insidious form of fear is that which masquerades as common sense or even wisdom, condemning as foolish, reckless, insignificant, or futile the small daily acts of courage which help to preserve a person's self-respect and inherent human dignity."

Martin Luther King, Jr. gave us all a reason to dream.

What will it be?

"Love, compassion, and tolerance are necessities, not luxuries. Without them humanity will not survive."

~ **The 14th Dalai Lama**

74.   BEING YOU

> "The most important kind of freedom is to be what you really are.
> If you trade in your reality for a role, you give up your ability to feel,
> and in exchange, put on a mask."
>
> ~ **Jim Morrison**

*A*s humans, embedded in the fabric of mystery, every moment is raw and original. We are in an open circumstance of unfathomable complexity. In other words, the stakes are so high, we have nothing to lose, really. The canvas is ours, should we choose to play and paint our freedom.
And what is our freedom? How do we know it and feel it?

> "Freedom: ...a roaring of ...contradictions...
> inconsistencies: life." Tristan Tzara's words sing
> to the unlimited range of possibilities.

Whatever you do be Bold.
Be provocative.
Be dangerous.
Take risks.
Quit your job. Love for a living. Do nothing.
Become a nun. Paint your house pink.
Meditate out of your cage. Adopt a child.
Upset the status quo of your own (dis-) comfort.
Turn your life into a surrealistic dream.
Go broke breaking the bonds that drain you of your daring.
Wash away that which wears you down.
Get rid of toxic energy.
Truth is the greatest healer.

Either own your part and grow together,
or state your truth and walk.

"Sometimes you just gotta let shit go and say
to 'hell with it' and move on."

~ Eminem

"If I could only give three words of advice," Randy Pausch tells us in his Last Lecture before his passing, "They would be, "Tell the Truth." If I got three more words I'd add, "All the time."

And I'd add three more: "Just be you."

And if you don't like what you see, change is possible if you define it as possible.

As Marshall McLuhan once said, "Men
[and women] on frontiers, whether of time or
space, abandon their previous identities."

Step out of fear. Be new — raw, shaky, original, you.

"There is vitality, a life force, a quickening that is translated through you into action," Martha Graham writes in illuminating the heart of originality. "And because there is only one of you in all of time, this expression is unique. And if you block it, it will never exist through any other medium and it will be lost. The world will not have it. It is not your business to determine how good it is nor how valuable nor how it compares with other expressions. It is your business to keep it yours clearly and directly, to keep the channel open ...keep yourself open and aware to the urges that motivate you. ... No artist is pleased ...There is only a queer divine dissatisfaction, a blessed unrest that keeps us marching and makes us more alive..."

"Undermining your authenticity by succumbing to someone else's second thoughts is a sinister, subtle, and seductive form of self-abuse," Sarah Ban Breathnach reminds us.

And let us remember the eternal wisdom of Mark Twain when he said, "A discriminating irreverence is the creator and protector of human liberty."

In other words, embody your wild crazy
beauty and get on with being you.

75. HOLY LONGING

> "Every living creature gets about a billion heartbeats worth of life.
> Small animals just consume their lives faster."
>
> ~ **Jonah Leher**

*D*eath is not a rumor. There are no exceptions.

"The most intractable of our experiences," Aldous Huxley tells us, "is our experience of Time — the intuition of duration, combined with the thought of perpetual perishing."

But why be distressed over discontinuity?

Ludwig Wittgenstein offers a point of view that addresses the question head on. He says, "Death is not an event in life: we do not live to experience death. If we take eternity to mean not infinite temporal duration but timelessness, then eternal life belongs to those who live in the present."

As the story goes, William James was once walking along a street in Cambridge, Massachusetts, accompanied by two of his students, a young man and woman. A large imposing figure, swinging his cane, talking to himself, oblivious to the others, approached them. Remarked the girl: "Whoever he is, he's the epitome of the absentminded professor." "What you really mean," said James, "is that he is present-minded somewhere else."

From such a non-local knowing that the 'now' isn't just 'here' but 'everywhere,' abandon the myopia of presence in the singular tense. We are multidimensional, finely functioning artists with a palette of infinite colors not merely in time but in memory as well. Travel wherever your fantasy takes you — it may be an unparalleled world, one that had been there all along, waiting to be inhabited in a whole new shapeshifting of selves still in chrysalis. Dive into expansive new expressions of being that excite and nurture the most meaningful, heart-centered, purpose of your life.

Goethe recognized the liberating-urge as a "holy longing," writing, "I praise what is truly alive, what longs to be burned to death. A strange feeling comes over you when you see the silent candle burning, a desire for higher love-making sweeps you upward, and, finally, insane for the light, you are the butterfly and you are gone. And so long as you haven't experienced this: to die and so to grow, you are only a troubled guest on this dark earth."

"We are here to laugh... [and] live our lives so well, that Death trembles to take us," declares Charles Bukowski.

Are we living our lives so well that "death will tremble to take us?"

Or does it require a change of attitude or a life change, or both?.

Or, something totally other?

What is your 'holy longing?'

"This is the highest wisdom that I own; freedom and life are earned by those alone who conquer them each day anew."

~ Goethe

76.   UNIFYING LIBERTY

*W*e all know, deep down inside, that love doesn't begin or end upon the lips of a lover, any more than a war begins or ends on a battlefield, or a city street. True love and lasting peace must come from a radical change of heart. Aung San Suu Kyi offers insight into what that means: "A revolution of the spirit begins by first learning how to liberate our own minds from fear, apathy, and ignorance."

Chögyal Namkhai Norbu, a renowned Tibetan Buddhist teacher explains the process of 'self-liberation,' saying, "Whatever manifests in the field of experience...is allowed to arise just as it is, without judgment of it as good or bad, beautiful or ugly. And in that same moment, if there is no clinging, or attachment, without effort, or even volition, whatever it is that arises, whether as a thought or as an external event, automatically liberates itself, by itself. Practicing in this way the seeds of...dualistic vision [giving rise to fear, apathy, and ignorance] never even get a chance to sprout, much less to take root and grow. So the practitioner lives his or her life in an ordinary way, without needing any rules other than his and her own awareness, but always remaining in the state of primordial unity by integrating his and her state with whatever arises as part of their experience, and with absolutely nothing to be seen outwardly to show that [they are] practicing. This is what is meant by self-liberation...."

And then we are faced with the ultimate challenge of *unifying liberty* — from 'my' freedom to 'our' freedom. Nelson Mandela stated it this way: "I found that I could not even enjoy the poor and limited freedoms I was allowed [in prison] when I knew my people were not free. Freedom is indivisible; the chains on any one on my people were the chains on all of them, the chains on all of them were the chains on me."

"I am because we are. We are because I am."

~ African proverb

77.　　LOVING HUMILITY

"Ring the bells that still can ring. Forget your perfect offering.
There is a crack in everything. That's how the light gets in."

~ **Leonard Cohen**

I ask myself as often as I need to: Can I renew my courage to love? Can I be in communion with myself, others, and the world, simultaneously?

"All my life, I have been driven by one dream, one goal, one vision: To overthrow a farm labor system in this nation that treats farm workers as if they were not important human beings," Cesar Chavez said in declaring his life's work. "Farm workers are not agricultural implements. They are not beasts of burden to be used and discarded. [Although] we are suffering," he goes on to say, "we are not afraid to suffer in order to win our cause. [In fact], "we draw our strength from the very despair in which we have been forced to live. We shall endure."

We *are* in this together.

We need each other to actualize our full potential to love, our full potential to liberate ourselves and each other, together, as we evolve LIFE — a future to believe in.

Kahlil Gibran tells us, "I have learned silence from the talkative, tolerance from the intolerant and kindness from the unkind."

Dostoyevsky informs us of the power of "human love," saying, "At some ideas you stand perplexed, especially at the sight of human sins, uncertain whether to combat it by force or by human love. Always decide, 'I will combat it with human love.' If you make up your mind about that once and for all, you can conquer the whole world. *Loving humility* is a terrible force; it is the strongest of all things and there is nothing like it."

William Carlos Williams asks, "What power has love but forgiveness?"

In other words, by its intervention what has been done can be undone.

What good is it otherwise?

> "We must always seek to ally ourselves with that part of the enemy that knows what is right."
>
> ~ **Mahatma Gandhi**

"Piet Fourie and his brutal warders were mere cogs in the racial machine of apartheid," writes Ahmed Kathrada in his book *A Simple Freedom*. "They were characters who should be looked upon with pity, not hate," he continues. "When the dust of conflict and struggle and bloodshed settled they were still going to be with us. They, and those who were guilty of indoctrinating them to believe that we were inferior beings, could not be drowned in the sea. We were going to strive to win them over and join in the building of a new, non-racial, democratic South Africa. Hate must give way to forgiveness and reconciliation. There is no other way."

I ask myself, who can I forgive today?

And how might I express that forgiveness?

78. AN INVINCIBLE SUMMER

Aung San Suu Kyi said that during her years of solitary
incarceration that she learned her "most precious
lesson" from a poem by Rabindranath Tagore.

"*If* they answer not your call, walk alone: If they are afraid
and cower mutely facing the wall, O Thou of evil luck, open
the mind and speak out alone. If they turn away and desert
you when crossing the wilderness, O Thou of evil luck,
trample the thorns under the tread, and along the blood-
lined track travel alone. If they do not hold up the light
when the night is troubled with storm, O Thou of evil luck,
with the thunder-flame of pain ignite thine own heart, and let
it burn alone."

"There are no words of comfort in the poem," she continued.
"No assurances of joy and peace at the end of the harsh
journey. There is no pretense that it is anything but evil luck
to receive no answer to your call, to be deserted in the middle
of the wilderness, to have no one who would hold up a light
to aid you through a stormy night. It is not a poem that offers
heart's ease, but it teaches you that a citadel of endurance can
be built on a foundation of anguish. How can anybody who
has learnt to ignite his heart with the thunder flame of his
own pain ever know defeat?

"Victory is ensured to those who are capable of learning
the hardest lessons that life has to offer," she concluded.

In speaking about the modern hero and heroine Joseph
Campbell informs us: "The modern hero, the modern

individual who dares to heed the call and seek the mansion of that presence with whom it is our whole destiny to be atoned, cannot, indeed must not, wait for his community to cast off its slough of pride, fear, rationalized avarice, and sanctified misunderstanding. 'Live,' Nietzsche says, 'as though the day were here.' It is not society that is to guide and save the creative hero, but precisely the reverse. And so every one of us shares the supreme ordeal and carries the cross of the redeemer — not in the bright moments of his tribe's great victories, but in the silences of his personal despair."

George Santayana writes, "A string of excited, fugitive, miscellaneous pleasures is not happiness; happiness resides in imaginative reflection and judgment, when the picture of one's life, or of human life, as it truly has been or is, satisfies the will, and is gladly accepted."

When can the will be satisfied?

When it has been well worked.

When it has tested itself against the necessary resistance of the world.

Against ignorance, against doubt, against hopelessness.

It needs the jagged edge of hardship, to even know it exists, and then work the wonders it longs to make real.

> "In the depth of winter, I finally learned that within me there lay an invincible summer."
>
> ~ **Albert Camus**

79.   THINK. FEEL. ACT.

"Map new terrain rather than chart old landmarks."

~ Marshall McLuhan

The dharma intelligence guiding our awakening is another way of talking about awareness creatively fused with every quality of heart that we consider valuable in actualizing freedom and peace. Taken together, this is our instinct for freedom — the natural urge of the heart to trust itself — a core knowingness that is both beneath and inclusive of projections and expectations, personas and defenses, and every other compromising trick of the mind and veil of self-deception. Saint Catherine of Sienna declared her devotion to liberation this way: "My being is god. Not by simple participation, but by a true transformation of my being."

Sophrosyne is a Greek philosophical term for 'moral sanity' and from there self control or moderation guided by true self-knowledge. In other words, "care and intelligence in conducting one's life; a tempered balance and wisdom."

This balanced wisdom is an intuitive flow of liberating presence that keeps freeing us everyday, in every way, which allows us to feel life as it is — in its raw merciless beauty.

Gregory David Roberts, author of *Shantaram*, offers us a glimpse into his sense of what it means to be human, walking on the landscape of the imperfect present.

"Put one foot forward and then the other," he begins.
"Lift our eyes to the snarl and smile of the world..."

"Think. Feel. Act."

"Add our little consequence to the tides of good and evil that flood and drain the world.

"Drag our shadowed crosses into the hope of another night. Push our brave hearts into the promise of a new day. With love: the passionate search for truth other than our own. With longing: the pure, ineffable yearning to be saved."

"For so long as fate keeps waiting, we live on," he continues. "God help us. God forgive us. We live on."

> Maya Angelou tell us "We cannot change the past,
> but we can change our attitude toward it.
> Uproot guilt and plant forgiveness.

> "Tear out arrogance and seed humility. Exchange
> love for hate — thereby, making the present
> comfortable and the future promising."

80. THE ARCHETYPAL REVOLUTION

"Those who say that spirituality has nothing to do with politics do not
know what spirituality really means."

~ **Mahatma Gandhi**

Like a lot of people who care about something passionately
and intimately, the more deeply I entered the crisis in Burma,
the more I both personalized it and projected it beyond one
country's crisis alone. The struggle for freedom in Burma
became the archetypal revolution that every nation and every
person encounters every day — the struggle to understand
right and wrong, love and fear, truth and ignorance, in one's
own heart.

As the psychological membrane between me — the American
spiritual activist — and them — the oppressed people of
Burma — disappeared, it was as if I was feeling my own
family being tortured and killed. Many times it was unclear
whether to bless or curse the fate that had first drawn me to
that distant land.

However, over time, the crisis in Burma compelled me to
merge the largely intuitive processes of self-transformation,
the evolution of freedom, and the experience of conscience,
with the complex world of politics, propaganda, international
relations, environmental sanity, activism, and global human
rights.

Aung San Suu Kyi once told me that "spirituality and
politics cannot be separated, ultimately. Both deal with the

everyday life of people. And at the core of life — at the core of spirituality and politics — are the same qualities, that of human freedom and human dignity."

Awakening one's own unique expression of *world dharma* consists of liberating actions manifested over a lifetime, actions that include honoring our small, (and easily dismissed) triumphs along the way.

The *dharma* is a way of life,' not a process to
complete. Align with the little joys found in
little changes, whatever they may be.

A political prisoner in Burma once told me how he brought the *dharma* into his prison cell. He said that he recited the following words every day during his many years of incarceration, as a means to keep his spiritual world and *dharma* activism alive, even when alone in a dark cell:

'Motivated by loving kindness, I commit myself to
helping others. With open-handed generosity, I joyously
share my time, ideas, and resources with others.

'With stillness, simplicity, and contentment, I openly
offer my presence in thought, word, and deed to
others. With truthful communication, I commit
myself to speech that uplifts the lives of others.

'With mindfulness clear and radiant, I dedicate myself
to making my country and the world a better place.'

"There is no force that can put an end to the human quest for freedom."

~ Liu Xiao

According to its charter, The United Nations was founded "to reaffirm faith in fundamental human rights, in the dignity and worth of the human person, in the equal rights of men and women and of nations large and small."

"Freedom from fear" could be said to sum up the whole philosophy of human rights."

~ **Dag Hammarskjold**

81.   THERE IS A TIME

> "You are something the whole universe is doing in the same way that a wave is something the whole ocean is doing."
>
> ~ Alan Watts

*A*ung San Suu Kyi and her colleagues in Burma opened me up to the wisdom of a whole world view, the awakening of a *world dharma*. Not only did they emphasize how every aspect of existence was interrelated, they stressed the importance of everyday action — daily deeds directed toward the greater good.

In one conversation Aung San Suu Kyi emphasized how everyone could consciously participate in bringing about change, saying, "As spiritual and political beings we are all activists at heart. No one is outside of society. Not even the monks and nuns. Our revolution includes them. It is about our freedom. That means everybody. We must see that nothing and no one is separate from this freedom. No one is an island in this world."

William R. Catton, Jr., the environmental sociologist, addresses the issue from another angle, stating: "Our lifestyles, mores, institutions, patterns of interaction, values, and expectations are shaped by a cultural heritage that was formed in a time when carrying capacity exceeded the human load. A cultural heritage can outlast the conditions that produced it. That carrying capacity surplus is gone now, eroded both by population increase and immense technological enlargement of per capita resource appetites and environmental impacts. Human life is now being lived in an era of deepening carrying capacity deficit. All of the familiar aspects of human societal life are under compelling pressure to change in this new era when the load increasingly exceeds the carrying capacities of many local regions — and of a finite planet."

"It's a measure of the depth of our consumer trance that the death of the planet is not sufficient to break it."

~ Kalle Lasn

William Catton, Jr. goes onto say, "It is axiomatic that we are in no way protected from the consequences of our actions by remaining confused about the ecological meaning of our humanness, ignorant of ecological processes, and unmindful of the ecological aspects of history."

U. S. President Barack Obama said it this way: "The issue of climate change is one that we ignore at our own peril....we can be scientifically certain...that our continued use of fossil fuels is pushing us to a point of no return. And unless we free ourselves from a dependence on these fossil fuels and chart a new course on energy..., we are condemning future generations to global catastrophe."

In other words, "Some things [we] must always be unable to bear," William Faulkner reminds us. "Some things [we] must never stop refusing to bear. Injustice and outrage and dishonor and shame. No matter what, refuse to bear them."

"There is a time when the operation of the machine becomes so odious, makes you so sick at heart," the American political activist Mario Savio so famously said, "that you can't take part; you can't even passively take part. And you've got to put your bodies upon the gears and upon the wheels, upon the levers, upon all the apparatus and you've got to make it stop."

"The greatest threat to humanity and peace is not corruption and evil; the greatest threat is the mass of people who watch it and do absolutely nothing about it."

~ Albert Einstein

82.   GREAT THANKS

The moment our awareness goes beyond our own self-interest and begins to care about others as an extension of ourselves, the heart will inevitably be forced to assimilate many new dimensions. It's one thing to discover oneself through oneself but it's another thing altogether to transform oneself through relationships.

The path of 'mutual caring' is one of heartbreak and high stakes. It means that we are willing to forego personal comfort for the sake of opening our hearts to the cries and sorrows of the world.

Of course, it's easy to talk about 'embracing the world as an extension of self,' but to lift the veil of separation even a little and to actually feel what's going on in and around us, is an act of enormous courage. This awakening can be likened to the dedication of good parents who are willing to do anything to nurture and safeguard their children.

Caring is foremost in their minds.

In the same way, as our sphere of love and compassion expands beyond our own blood, we embrace a larger and more diverse circle of life.

Can we imagine feeling such a deep heart bond for all life?

"We have to acknowledge that there is a radical difference between a secular and a sacred manner of being in the world," states Sam Keen. "In the 21st century we will have to learn to cherish all creatures in the commonwealth of sentient beings if we are going to preserve our fragile environment."

The Astronomer, Carl Sagan, while pointing
to an image of the Earth taken from the
Jupiter space craft 367 million miles away,
exclaimed: "Look at that dot.

"That's here. That's home. That's us."

"On it everyone you love, everyone you know, everyone you ever heard of, every human being who ever was, lived out their lives. The aggregate of our joy and suffering, thousands of confident religions, ideologies, and economic doctrines, every hunter and forager, every hero and coward, every creator and destroyer of civilization, every king and peasant, every young couple in love, every mother and father, hopeful child, inventor, and explorer, every teacher of morals, every corrupt politician, every saint and sinner in the history of our species lived there — on a mote of dust suspended in a sunbeam."

"Great thanks are due to Nature for putting into the life
of each being so much healing power," Goethe once said.

What is the healing power we have in our hands today?

How will we use it?

"I define enlightenment as the depth to which one sees the oneness of life, the interconnectedness of life. And the degree of your enlightenment can be measured by your actions."

~ Roshi Bernie Glassman

83.   EVERY HOUR IS GRACE

"We must learn to regard people less in light of what they do
or omit to do, and more in the light of what they suffer."

~ Dietrich Bonhoeffer

Accepting the pure emotion of being human without protective personas or defenses shrouding our hearts — is perhaps the greatest challenge one can face.

Beyond the moments of life's joyful radiance, opening ourselves to feel the 'whole' is often overwhelming. The torment we see in the faces on our computer screens and television screens is staggering. The sight of the homeless suffering on our city streets shudders the senses. To feel the anguish that at times comes with deep personal relationships can be debilitating.

But there it is, always before our eyes and in our hearts, and if our desire for liberation is to encompass the world, we must risk feeling otherness as a deeply intimate aspect of ourselves.

Toni Morrison says it this way:

"Beloved, you are my sister, You are my daughter, You are my face; You are me."

"For me, every hour is grace," Elie Wiesel tells us." And I feel gratitude in my heart each time I can meet someone and look at his or her smile."

> And if I were you and you were me, how might
> we conduct ourselves differently today?

84. ONE PERSON AT A TIME

"Because we all share an identical need for love," The 14th Dalai Lama tells us, "it is possible to feel that anybody we meet, in whatever circumstances, is a brother or sister."

*C*an you imagine what it would feel like to love one hundred people as intensely and intimately as you would your lover, your wife, your husband, or your children? If it were even possible to command our hearts at will to open to all of humankind that widely, would we last a month, a week, an hour, a minute?

In other words, the idealism of compassionately embracing the world must be tempered with the wisdom to go slowly — *one person at a time.*

"If I look at the mass, I will never act," Mother Teresa said. "If I look at one, I will."

"I've learned that people will forget what you said, people will forget what you did, but people will never forget how you made them feel."

~ Maya Angelou

85.   OUR CONSCIENCE

"Never do anything against conscience even if the state demands it."

~ Albert Einstein

*C*onscience is the soul of consciousness and the basis of our worth as a human being. Listening to conscience is to discern what is real and good from what is unreal and not beneficial. This process continually nourishes our *dharma intelligence,* strengthens our integrity and dignity, and provides fertile ground for our ethical identity to grow and expand into a canopy of compassion that covers the whole of life.

Learning to respond to conscience is in itself a conscious art, an expression of inner activism that serves to both empower one's own most benevolent presence and guide us in finding liberation through living, in whatever the circumstances may be.

Honoring conscience is the embodiment of dignity, freedom itself.

Aung San Suu Kyi speaks to the 'power of conscience' saying, "As I travel through my country [of Burma], people often ask me how it feels to have been imprisoned in my home — first for six years, then for 19 months [and now after seven additional years she was released on Nov 13, 2010]. How could I stand the separation from family and friends? It is ironic, I say, that in an authoritarian state it is only the prisoner of conscience who is genuinely free. Yes, we have given up our right to a normal life. But we have stayed true to that most precious part of our humanity — our conscience."

Conscience, choice, and freedom grow from one another and, in so doing, perpetuate a cycle of freedom. The more freedom one has, the greater the perspective on life. The more space; the more responsibility we feel about taking part in the lives of others. From there the stakes get higher and the decisions more complex. Our responsibility increases.

Essentially, conscience asks that we care about life, and wisdom tells us to act.

"Our lives begin to end the day we become silent about things that matter."
~ Martin Luther King Jr.

It was Vaclav Havel who said, "We live in a postmodern world, where everything is possible and almost nothing is certain....The planetary civilization to which we all belong confronts us with global challenges. We stand helpless before them because our civilization has essentially globalized only the surface of our lives. But our inner self continues to have a life of its own. And the fewer answers the era of rational knowledge provides to the basic questions of human being, the more deeply it would seem that people, behind its back as it were, cling to the ancient certainties of their tribe."

"The greatest glory of a free-born people," William Harvard wrote, "is to transmit that freedom to their children."

To challenge the centrifugal force of our inner tribalism, Desmond Tutu reminds us that human rights are protected by awakening conscience, stating that "Our religious and philosophical teachings tell us that human suffering anywhere must be accepted as our own suffering. And our worldly experience convinces us that only practical political action can help end that suffering."

Liberty = autonomy = immunity from the arbitrary exercise of authority = political independence, freedom of choice; to think or feel or do as one pleases; personal freedom from servitude or confinement or oppression.

"I am free, no matter what rules surround me. If I find them tolerable, I tolerate them; if I find them too obnoxious, I break them. I am free because I know that I alone am morally responsible for everything I do."

~ **Robert A. Heinlein**

86.　THE SACRED MYSTERY

*I*s it possible, more important, or acceptable, to allow yourself to frolic in joy while you know the world is ablaze with hatred, ignorance, and war? Is it possible to let in the suffering — the collapse of peoples lives, the degradation of our planet — and at the same time relax enough to enjoy ordinary human happiness? Can we embrace an awareness of this world — the harsh truth of its complexities — without any spin at all? Can we allow for the fact that it's a bitter, brutal landscape for the majority of people, who, at this very moment, are struggling to survive in the most incomprehensible circumstances? Can we live a normal life knowing that these people are our relatives and we are here to help?

The 14th Dalai Lama provides us with his answer: "In today's highly interdependent world, individuals and nations can no longer resolve many of their problems by themselves. We need one another. We must therefore develop a sense of universal responsibility to protect and nurture the global family, to support its weaker members and to preserve and tend to the environment in which we all live."

Shantideva, an 8th century Buddhist mystic illuminated the transformational power of what he called the *sacred mystery* — the exchanging of oneself for others. He called this awakening "the Way of the Bodhisattva," and considered it the finest path for transforming oneself while simultaneously providing a 'liberating mirror' for others to potentially see themselves more clearly. His profound attitude was expressed in the simplest way, stating: "Whenever I catch sight of others, by thinking, 'It is through them, that I will reach awakening,' I'll look with sincerity and love."

To develop love and compassion let us consider following the *sacred mystery* of 'exchanging oneself for others,' and practice making another's suffering our own.

As such, allow our hearts to quiver.
Allow them to be touched.
Allow them to open.

Pause, and feel the actual sensations of their emotional and psychological being as our own. If fear arises, challenge it. If sorrow arises, challenge it too.

Challenge any thought or emotion that suggests that it's wrong or that it's too much or that you have something better to do.

Remain steadfast in your presence.
Feel the situation as a sacred opportunity —
for your own liberation and potentially, theirs too.

"When we come into contact with the other person," Thich Nhat Hanh tells us, "our thoughts and actions should express our mind of compassion, even if that person says and does things that are not easy to accept. We practice in this way until we see clearly that our love is not contingent upon the other person being lovable."

Ram Dass states it this way: "Remember the bottom line: We're here to awaken from the illusion of separateness. As we meet, as we speak out, a consciousness of unity is quietly there, at the heart of our action. We call on it, in fact we look for it, in whatever comes up. And we do so not because it's useful, or generous, or conciliatory, but because it's true. Unity has to be what's most real in consciousness if it's going to have power in action. Ultimately, it's got to be what we 'are'."

Ask yourself, what can be done to ease
this person's pain, their struggle?

What can I do to help?
As concretely as possible.
In this very moment, now.

"I have not come to resolve anything. I have come to sing and for you to sing with me," please.

~ **Pablo Neruda**

87.   LIGHTING THE SKY

"If you wish to be loved, love."

~ **Seneca**

*W*hether we admit it or not, everyone wants to be touched — physically, emotionally, and spiritually. Everyone wants to be loved, to be heard, to feel special. How beautiful it is to be with someone who genuinely adores you. They celebrate you and draw out the most gorgeous, evocative places in your heart and mind.

Imagine offering our beauty — freely, and being someone who is joyously willing to 'give' the love they seek; to 'BE' the chemistry they long for; to be that alive, that creatively authentic — right now.

Vincent van Gogh said, "I feel that there is nothing more truly artistic than to love people."

> "The sun never says to the earth, 'You owe me.'
> Look what happens with a love like that.
> It lights the whole Sky."
>
> ~ **Hafiz**

88. NATURAL MUTUALITY

"Friends can help each other. A true friend is someone who lets you have total freedom to be yourself — and especially to feel. Or, not feel. Whatever you happen to be feeling at the moment is fine with them. That's what real love amounts to — letting a person be what he [and she] really is."

~ Jim Morrison

What entering 'shared space' actually means as beloved or friends is for each of us to discover. When separation dissolves, 'my presence' and 'your presence,' converge. Relationship in that moment becomes a liberating dance of creativity, communion, daring — a shared original goodness — rather than a solo act of 'me being aware of me, alone,' while being 'aware of you, over there.'

We let go, without losing our autonomy, our identity, our integrity, giving ourselves full permission to feel our way in, together, rather than 'observing, witnessing, or mirroring phenomena,' alone.

"I'll let you be in my dreams if I can be in yours."

~ Bob Dylan

Occupying *natural mutuality* removes the need for a transcendent agenda.

It brings us into the moment for no other purpose than to be together.

And that togetherness doesn't even have
to be particularly spiritual.

Naturalness is enough.

"If you really want to make a friend, go to someone's house and eat with
them...The people who give you their food give you their heart."

~ **Cesar Chavez**

89.   A KISS

Can we embrace the whole of our being, not as an ideal but as an experience of expansion, inclusion, and dimension?

This includes ambiguity and uncertainty.
It also includes reality — physical reality and desire.
Let us not forget that we are embodied Beings —
Lusty, Delicious, Desirable.

"Have you ever lost yourself in a kiss?" the poet and spoken word artist Saul Williams asks. "I mean pure psychedelic inebriation. Not just lustful petting but transcendental metamorphosis when you became aware that the greatness of this being was breathing into you. Licking the sides and corners of your mouth...with the essence of your passionate being and then opened by the same mouth and delivered back to you, over and over again — the first kiss of the rest of your life. A kiss that confirms that the universe is aligned, that the world's greatest resource is love, and maybe even that God is a woman."

> "Sex and beauty are inseparable, like life and consciousness.
> And the intelligence which goes with sex and beauty,
> and arises out of sex and beauty, is intuition."
>
> ~ D.H. Lawrence

90.   INHERENT SANCTITY

There's no predetermined course of action that will assure our authenticity. That would be like someone telling us what a 'real orgasm' should feel like. Should it be transpersonal or personal? Should it be Buddhist, atheist, or Jewish? Should it be self-involved or should it be absent of self? Should I be mindful of my orgasm or should I lose myself in it completely? Should I worry about mine, or my lack of one, or should I see myself as natural? Should I be thinking when I am having one, or should a real one take me beyond thought? Am I being spiritual when I have one or avoiding my higher self? The ways in which we discriminate between this or that are endless. Seeking spiritual correctness is a thankless job. And one in which you will always be graded by a lie: your own unwillingness to be you — human — reinventing (or faking) 'correctness' every moment.

> Trust in the inherent sanctity of your most
> genuine expression of self and live it.

The legendary singer-songwriter, Tom Waits, tells a simple story about the wisdom of accepting our unique nature. "My kids are starting to notice I'm a little different from the other dads," Waits explains. 'Why don't you have a straight job like everyone else?' they asked me the other day. I told them this story: In the forest, there was a crooked tree and a straight tree. Every day, the straight tree would say to the crooked tree, "Look at me...I'm tall, and I'm straight, and I'm handsome. Look at you...you're all crooked and bent over. No one wants to look at you." And they grew up in that forest together.

"And then one day the loggers came, and they saw the crooked tree and the straight tree, and they said, "Just cut the straight trees and leave the rest."

"So the loggers turned all the straight trees into lumber and toothpicks and paper. And the crooked tree is still there, growing stronger and stranger every day."

"Just trust yourself then you will know how to live."

~ Johann Wolfgang von Goethe

91. THE SMILE

"I used to live in a room full of mirrors; all I could see was me.
I take my spirit and I crash my mirrors, now the whole world is
here for me to see."

~ Jimi Hendrix

*O*ne doesn't discover freedom, one presumes it, breathes it, lives it.

Freedom is instinctual.

It's beyond qualifications, outcomes, and strategies.

It's expressed exactly in the same way we smile.

Can you engage life as naturally as you smile?

When we smile, we are, for a moment, free from conflict. Our awareness and presence are dedicated to a natural expression of intimacy. The dilemma of looking into the past or the future for some idea of a resolution to the present is gone, through the timeless tenderness offered by the smile itself.

Can you abandon yourself to life that fully, and really know that and freedom are identical to living a spiritual life?

"i thank You God for this amazing day: for the leaping greenly spirits
of trees and a blue true dream of sky; and for everything which
is natural which is infinite which is yes."

~ e. e. cummings

92.   A FULL BREATH

The wisdom of actualizing the 'natural life' sees that there is no indestructible realization to seek, no final solution to existence, no goal of life, and no required insight apart from the ability to be true to yourself and respectful of others. To this end, there is no spirituality to seek. It is what is, the very nature of life. It is as innate to existence as the breath. One doesn't need to learn to breathe. One doesn't need to become more spiritual or less material.

We only need to be inspired to do something remarkable with the vitality a full breath provides us.

> "Anxiety is the dizziness of freedom."
> ~ **Kierkegaard**

At one point, as a monk, I began to obsess about getting my sitting meditation posture 'perfectly right' — back straight, legs just right, knees touching the floor, head tilted slightly, poised, balanced, with long, slow, deep breaths. The more I tried, the more detailed I became. I often compared myself to the five-hundred or so other monks in the meditation hall. This went on until I had actually 'perfected' it. Now, I said to myself, 'I can get on with the business of achieving 'perfect realization.'

The only problem was that my perfect posture was much more painful than my most natural one.

So what did I spend all that time for — it was a form of 'perfect' that wasn't practical. Once I dropped the picture I was able to the return to the greater issue, understanding the difference between natural freedom and perfect posturing.

Natural freedom arises out of an abiding respect for our imperfect wholeness. Who needs to be perfect when you can be human?

So, natural freedom is that condition of being that precedes ideas of liberation; it undermines dogmas, doctrines, mythologies, self-images, attainments, contracts with perfection, and all other inherited forms of self-protection and self-enhancement.

Natural freedom precedes these self-delusions, but it also exceeds them. It is a paradoxical and inclusive sense of being. Simply said, natural freedom is the ability to live and die right now with a shameless sense of goodness and beauty.

We are human, so let nothing human be foreign to us.

93. HEALTH FOR HUMANITY

"Violence can only be concealed by a lie,"
Aleksandr Solzhenitsyn informs us. "And the
lie can only be maintained by violence."

*W*hat fashions itself between spontaneous local beauty and the innate intelligence of the cosmos is the interrelated fabric of our social and political world. In order to discover the 'way of life' that most inspires us, we must each wake up to our inner responsibility as a social and political being. This means opening our eyes to the world that surrounds us. It means looking at the inequities and misfortunes that force people to live on the streets of our neighborhoods. It means standing up to the blind logic of aggressive militarization that global powers are currently forcing upon distant nations and millions of innocent lives.

We should not turn away from that suffering.

"Nationalism of one kind or another was the cause of most of the genocide of the twentieth century. Flags are bits of colored cloth that governments use first to shrink-wrap people's brains and then as ceremonial shrouds to bury the dead."

~ **Arundhati Roy**

Eunice Wong, in her essay *The Great Forgetting*, reminds us of the importance of coming out of the coma of cultural amnesia that feeds apathy, denial, and ignorance. "The Smithsonian National Museum of the American Indian, located on the Mall in Washington, D.C., is a monument to historical amnesia," she states. "The blond limestone building, surrounded by indigenous crops of corn, tobacco and squash, invites visitors on a guilt-free, theme park tour of Native American history, where acknowledgment of the American genocide is in extremely bad taste...We are molded as much by the histories we stifle as by the myths we create to exalt ourselves.

"Those who ignore the truth about their past are condemned to replicate, over and over, their crimes," she goes onto say. "The devastation in Iraq is the legacy of lessons unlearned, from the genocide of Native Americans, to slavery, to the Mexican war, to the invasion of Cuba and the Philippines, to Vietnam. America's brutal cycle of imperial invasion and occupation is as enduring as the cultivated illusion of its goodness. And the first step toward breaking this cycle and exposing this illusion is facing our history and ourselves. The National Museum of the American Indian feeds the mass amnesia that makes our national psychosis possible."

"The truth is cruel [at times]," George Santayana states,
"but it can be loved, and it makes free
those who have loved it."

"I am thankful I cannot forget. Because, as Native American writer
Paula Gunn Allen writes: 'the root of all oppression is the loss of memory.'
If this is true, health for humanity will come from never doing to others
what we wish to forget."

~ Alice Walker

94. LOVE IS AN ACTION

"It is repression that creates the revolutionary spirit of freedom."

~ Bobby Sands, Volunteer of the Provisional Irish Republican Army and member of the United Kingdom Parliament who died on the 66th day of a hunger strike while in HM Prison Maze.

"*Love is an action*, not just a state of mind," Aung San Suu Kyi once said. "It is not enough to just sit there and send thoughts of loving kindness.

One must get up and do something. Put that love into action," she declares.

"Those of us who decided to work for democracy in Burma made our choice in the conviction that the danger of standing up for basic human rights in a repressive society was preferable to the safety of a quiescent life in servitude," Aung San Suu Kyi goes onto to say. "Ours is a nonviolent movement that depends on faith in the human predilection for fair play and compassion. Some would insist that man is primarily an economic animal interested only in his material well-being. This is too narrow a view of a species which has produced numberless brave men and women who are prepared to undergo relentless persecution to uphold deeply held beliefs and principles. It is my pride and inspiration that such men and women exist in my country today."

The challenge of putting our love into action is always present. It's a living universe — waiting for each of us to evolve it — wisely, courageously, freely.

"The ultimate test of [person's] conscience may be his [and her] willingness to sacrifice something today for future generations whose words of thanks will not be heard."

~ **Gaylord Nelson, co-founder of Earth Day**

95. BRINGING ABOUT THE BEST

"Our species needs, and deserves a citizenry with minds wide awake and a basic understanding of how the world works."

~ Carl Sagan

*D*iscover the conviction that declares the difference between right and wrong, the difference between status quo and making things better. It is our task, right now, to find the inner certainty and direction to commit our whole being to bringing about the best our conscience has to offer.

"All the great things are simple, And ...
can be expressed in a single word: freedom..."

~ Winston Churchill

"Our availability to each other, our ability to dream each other's dreams and experience each other's biographies is part of the interpenetrating wave of the current time..." Jean Houston states. "We are being rescaled to planetary proportions, as we become resonant and intimate with our own depths."

On a simple level, we might consider how we consume, or how we discard waste, or emotions, or thoughts, or other people, or friendships; where do these go? What effect does our small daily habitual lack of awareness, as well as our real moments of mindfulness, have?

In what ways might these be challenged?

Martin Kovan shares his insight this way: "The old bent man who we see pass in slow-motion to the corner shop every day — it might make his day to receive a smile, a kind word. We ourselves can ride a bike to the shops, rather than drive. And consider how for the old man the days even of riding a bike are over. We can really appreciate this relative freedom to move. When we buy something, we could consider whether we really need it; instead of buying ourselves another un-needed thing, can we think of what someone else in our life might need?"

The joy in such reversals of focus, literally, transforms your immediate world. Of such shifts is real happiness made. Truth then comes to powerfully reside in the unremarkable details, as much as in our most cherished dreams.

Vaclav Havel, who spent years in prison for his activism in helping to bring freedom to his country, once said "Hope, in the deep and meaningful sense, is not the same as joy that things are going well, or willingness to invest in enterprises that are obviously headed for early success, but, rather, an ability to work for something because it is good, not just because it stands a chance to succeed.

"People who are used to seeing society only from above tend to be impatient," he continues. "They want to see immediate results. Anything that does not produce immediate results seems foolish. They don't have a lot of sympathy for acts which can only be evaluated years after they take place, which are motivated by moral factors, and therefore run the risk of never accomplishing anything."

"Freedom of expression is the foundation of human rights, the source of humanity and the mother of truth."

~ Liu Xiaobo, China's imprisoned Nobel Peace Laureate

96. RIGHT IN FRONT OF YOU

"Our character...is an omen of our destiny and the more integrity we have and keep, the simpler and nobler that destiny is likely to be."

~ George Santayana

During my first year as a monk in Burma, a dear friend, a Burmese monk named U Kundala, invited me to accompany him on a visit to his aged parents, both of whom lived in an old-age home on the outskirts of Rangoon. "I know just where my mother will be," he said in a tone of reverence as we walked into the compound. U Kundala smiled as he pointed to three old women seated on a bench beneath a large orange bougainvillea tree. He grabbed my hand as we walked hurriedly over to the women, introducing me first to his mother, Daw Khin Gyi.

After he and his mother spoke rapidly in Burmese for a minute or so, U Kundala invited me to join in. In halting Burmese I asked the three women their ages. They laughed. "Young men shouldn't ask old women their age," Daw Khin Gyi said. The fluency of her English startled me as much as her answer.

"I'm sorry," I said, "it's one of the only questions I know in Burmese."

"Well, I'm eighty-two, and my two friends are eighty and eighty-one. And you?" she asked curiously. "Thirty, my birthday was just a few months ago," I said.

"You're such a young man," she exclaimed. "What are you doing in Burma? Shouldn't you be married, enjoying yourself with your wife?"

Slightly taken aback, I looked toward U Kundala for reassurance, but he had walked off. "I'm a pongyi," I said, meaning that I was a monk. "I've been living at the *Mahasi* monastery with your son. I'm in your country to practice meditation and learn the *Dharma*. I'm not interested in marriage!" I concluded somewhat indignantly.

After a brief moment of silence Daw Khin Gyi asked in a curious voice, "Tell me, since you've become a monk, are you happy?"

"Yeah, sure," I replied without hesitation. "I'm happy. Well, you know...almost. You know how we Buddhists are, never really happy, but always just about there."

The women loved my comment and laughed uproariously. But instead of relaxing, I tensed. Her question made me think. Was I happy? What does that even mean?

I looked down at U Kundala's mother, who was staring at me intently, and I asked, "And you, are you happy?" No sooner had I finished the question than my heart dropped. I hadn't noticed that she was blind — her eyes were glazed, unblinking, with a texture of solid gray. Why hadn't U Kundala told me?

No wonder she didn't notice I was a monk.

As I was rebuking myself for asking such an insensitive question, and just about to apologize, she answered with a soft smile, "Yes, I am happy. Very happy. I have everything I need. Life is good."

It was hard to accept her contentment. Happiness in the best of circumstances seemed so elusive me. And happiness and blindness, in particular, seemed antithetical. All kinds of thoughts went through my head. Who would I be without sight? My entire existence was conditioned by my ability to see: my hopes, dreams, ambitions, and every identity I had about myself and life was tied into my ability to make contact with my eyes. I don't think I had ever considered how conditioned and interrelated my sense of being was until that moment — how utterly dependent I was. I took sight completely for granted, as well as the other senses, and mobility too.

"My friends tell me it's very beautiful here," she continued. "They describe the sunsets — the shades of color, even the stars and the moon, or sometimes a rainbow, or the flight of a bird. *My friends are my eyes.* But since I've nothing to compare it to it's more like listening to poetry than trying to visualize the scene. But for me beauty comes in other ways."

> "Wherever you look there is something to be seen."
>
> ~ Talmud

Her words themselves drifted in the air and seemed illuminated in the late morning sun. A space of being had opened in me beyond my normal awareness of just me. It was as if her words were compelling me to enter a shared space, such as the one she shared with her friends.

She broke my reflection with a kind smile and said, "I live simply. What do I need? I take my time when I walk. Where do I need to go? I have my walking stick. I have plenty of food. What more could I ask for? I have a bed in the shelter behind us. I sleep well at night. My clothes are few and comfortable. I stay clean, even though I'm very slow at bathing at the well. If I'm ill, we have herbal medicines."

She paused and turned toward me with a sincerity that melted the last strand of separation between us. "See, I have all I need," she said, "food, shelter, clothing, and medicines. In Burma we say, these are the four requisites for basic human happiness."

I hadn't noticed that U Kundala had walked up. Next to him was an elderly man bent over, standing with the aid of a cane. Daw Khin Kyi, sensing who it was, said something I didn't understand in Burmese. The old man sat next to her and they held each other's hands. She then looked up at me and said, "Please meet my husband, U Ohn Gyi."

And after a moment's pause said with a smile,
"By far the best thing for happiness is love."

97.   YOUR GUIDE

"We do not receive wisdom, we must discover it for ourselves, after
a journey through the wilderness, which no one else can make for us,
which no one can spare us, for our wisdom is the point of view from
which we come at last to regard the world."

~ Marcel Proust

There's no central plan of action for the next bold move.

Let the mysterious constellation of the whole universe, inside and outside, be your guide, your compass, Your Ultimate Teacher.

"To see a World in a Grain of Sand
A Heaven in a Wildflower
Hold Infinity in the Palm of your Hand
And Eternity in an Hour."

~ William Blake

98. REIGNITE DEDICATION

"If you assume that there's no hope, you guarantee that there will be no hope," Noam Chomsky writes. "If you assume that there is an instinct for freedom, that there are opportunities to change things, there's a chance you may contribute to making a better world. That's *your choice*."

There is an innate, transformational intelligence within each of us. It touches us in the ineffable language of the heart. We sense it as an intuitive pulse — a stirring perception that arouses us to make the unseen visible, bring clarity to the unknown, and ignite meaning in a world of limitless uncertainty.

Engaging the imperfect present means accepting the challenge to transform illusions and limitations. It's a courageous calling — rooted in awareness and reason and guided by conscience and compassion — that encourages our finest values and voices our greatest vision for all of humankind.

Freedom is our birthright.
It is our quest for existential authenticity.

Jean Houston writes, "Dear friends, we are assembled here for the purpose of inviting into our space-time collective a visible, tangible, audible manifestation of tomorrow. Tomorrow is here at this moment now, with us, among us, in us, but not quite born. Messages are coming to us all the time from tomorrow. It makes embryo noises to us through the most unlikely channels. Tomorrow aches to be born ... love is turning us into the next stage."

It is my belief that we are just beginning to understand the structures of consciousness and the nature of the Cosmos. We are children in the universe. This is our time on earth. Let us reignite the passion for what Joseph Campbell called "the soul's high Adventure." Let us enter life, evolving the highest intelligence possible, both individually and together.

> "Whatever you can do, or dream you can...begin it.
> "Boldness has genius, power and magic in it."
>
> **~ Goethe**

99. YOUR PRECIOUS LIFE

You — naked, mortal, uniquely free.

"*B*e in love with yr life," Jack Kerouac once said. "Be [a] crazy dumbsaint of the mind," he went onto say. "Blow as deep as you want to blow... Write what you want [to write]... [share your] ...unspeakable visions... [feel them] shivering in [your] chest, ...Believe in the holy contour of life... [have] No fear or shame in the dignity of yr experience... [be] In praise of Character in the Bleak inhuman Loneliness,... Composing wild, undisciplined, Pure [prose]... [and the] crazier the better... [and above all, remember]... You're a genius All the time."

Albert Schweitzer, with his characteristic simplicity and grace, said it in another way: "I am life which wills to live in the midst of life which wills to live."

"Doesn't everything die at last, and too soon?
Tell me, what do you plan to do
With [the rest of] your one wild and precious life?"

~ **Mary Oliver**

100.   AWAKE AWARE

"Liberty is the possibility of doubting, of making a mistake,...of searching and experimenting,... of saying No to any authority — literary, artistic, philosophical, religious, social, and even political."

~ Ignazio Silone

*O*n one of my final days in Burma, back in 1996, I met with U Kyi Maung, my eighty-year-old Burmese friend and mentor. As a freedom fighter in Burma's nonviolent revolution he had been imprisoned twice, spending eleven years in solitary confinement. I feared he would be rearrested at any moment. I asked him, "Sir, if you are re-arrested, what words would you like to leave for others to carry on the struggle for freedom?"

In a slow and reflective tone he replied, "For the coming generations I would emphasize two most important things: education and a deep sense of history. Knowledge is essential. They should learn about the world at large. This will assist them in shaping their own lives, freely. To grasp history is to grasp the importance of *interrelatedness* — the causes, conditions, and consequences of thought and action and how they affect the development or demise of civilization — human existence at large. Everyone plays a part.

The gift of life is to play that part with profound responsibility. "The 20th century has taught us great lessons in all aspects of human involvement. There have been some advances humankind could never have imagined. In this century we have seen the folly of ideologies, such as Fascism and

Communism, which are inconsistent with creativity and the flourishing of the spirit. From the 18th century came the rise of the British Empire that sent a plague of exploitation around the world. Yet it too was humbled.

"We have witnessed all types of conflict, from urban violence to global wars, from bolt-action rifles to the nuclear bomb, typewriters to computers, a revolution in music and dance. There's just so much, and within it all have come a few good men and women with vision, that remarkable gift to see our tomorrow today.

"Their gifts are renewing our hopes for the future of the planet, and our survival as a species. It's all about interrelatedness," he continued. "From its full exploration I believe will come the flourishing of civilization, and not its untimely demise."

He paused briefly. "As for me, don't worry. What I care about the most, and practice off and on throughout the day, is to be aware. That's all. To be aware.

"See, I have pieces of paper in my pockets that I carry with me: quotes, inspiring reminders. They refocus my mind on the here and now. That is the most important thing to me. To be present. Awake. Aware. My eleven years in prison were severe, but I used the time to my advantage. I never forget that what I am seeing now — that pale green line streaking across the pond, or the shadow of the tree across your leg — disappears the moment I turn my face. This is life's simplicity. Just the here and now. Aware that nothing is permanent.

"That barbed-wire fence across the back of Aung San Suu Kyi's compound over there — why worry about the presence of such an irritant? It's insignificant. Now if I worry about anything, it's that I might lose this sense of awareness. So I guard it as something precious. Things pass . . . that I have seen. Life is what you make it, now. So let us put our energies into life. Into understanding our interrelatedness. In this way I try not to lose my perspective."

I spent six months meeting with this wise statesman. I had bonded deeply with all he stood for, with Burma's struggle for freedom, and how their struggle "over there" is connected with our struggle for freedom "right here."

Later in the day, as he walked me to the door of his home, he said, "Don't worry. When death comes, let it come. What I do fear, however, is that I would be so weak that I would choose the easiest way out, to lie around in bed all day and read some book on the collapse of yet another totalitarian regime." We both laughed and said goodbye.

We both laughed and said goodbye.

101. DON'T SHUT YOUR EYES

"Let us put our heads together and see what life we will make for our children."

~ **Tatanka Iotanka (Sitting Bull, Lakota Leader)**

The awakening of consciousness is an opening process. It evolves much the same way as a flower opens to the sun. With light, soil, water, and air the flower gradually blossoms and emanates its natural fragrance. It is through relatedness that consciousness flowers, not through examining the darkness between the petals. For that reason, the art and activism of freedom and the emergence of a *world dharma* is an active engagement with the environment of our lives — self in relationship; self with other, self with the world, self with the cosmos.

"I have noticed even people who claim everything is predestined, and that we can do nothing to change it, look before they cross the road."

~ **Stephen Hawking**

Engage openly, artistically; empower your ability to expand into existence; bring awareness, color, richness, and beauty — and a liberating activism 'that stays alert' to any injustice to this life that we are all a part of.

> Aung San Suu Kyi once said, "We are either the enemies of progress or the friends of it. We are either takers, or givers. Creators or Destroyers."

"There is a story, which is fairly well known," Desmond Tutu writes, "about when the missionaries came to Africa.

They had the Bible and we, the natives, had the land. They said "Let us pray," and we dutifully shut our eyes. When we opened them, they now had the land and we had the Bible."

"Have you ever found yourself looking at a magazine cover, knowing that it wants you to feel like you're not pretty enough, thin enough, smart enough, rich enough? What if every time that happened, you just reached up and turned that magazine around? That's the challenge posed by the creator of the campaign don't shut your eyes, turn it around."

~ **Adbusters**

102. WE ARE EVERYWHERE

"Blessed are they who see beautiful things in humble places where other people see nothing."

~ Camille Pissarro

*M*other Teresa spoke to the heart of our humanness when she said, "We cannot do great things in life; we can only do small things with great love." And William James writes, "I am done with great things and big things, great institutions and big successes. I am for those tiny invisible molecular moral forces that work from individual to individual, creeping through the crannies of the world like so many rootlets, or like the capillary oozing of water, yet which if you give them time, will rend the hardest monuments of man's pride."

Enhancing the quality of our world — elevating the freedom of others, and sustaining our precious planet — will come from hundreds of millions of us performing the tiniest of thoughtful acts throughout the day, everyday, with the "great love" Mother Teresa speaks of. It is a selfless love born from caring; a love of life; a love of freedom, both our own and others', together as one.

"Mindful of his own dignity, he is mindful of others', because he wishes to safeguard what is in fact the essence of man's value, that no one is replaceable."

~ Eugene Ionesco

Freedom is non-local, WE are everywhere.

"The moon, ever a companion to me in prison, has grown more friendly with closer acquaintance," writes Jawaharlal Nehru, "a reminder of the loveliness of this world, of the waxing and waning of life, of light following darkness, of death and resurrection following each other in interminable succession. Every changing, yet ever the same, I have watched it in its different phases and its many moods in the evening as the shadows lengthen in the still hours of the night, and when the breath and whisper of dawn brings promise of the coming day."

In the final analysis, "Be kind," Philo states, "for everyone you meet is fighting a great battle."

103.   TO LIVE AND DIE

"I refuse to accept despair as a final response."

~ **Martin Luther King, Jr.**

*D*ays before I left Burma in 1996, I also met with my dear friend and mentor U Tin Oo. We had been Buddhist monks together in the early 1980s. He was now the chairman of the National League for Democracy, the political party of which Aung San Suu Kyi was the elected Prime Minister. I asked him what it took to emotionally and psychologically survive the severity of eleven years of prison and solitary confinement. His answer lives on as an essential guide to what it means to embrace the art and activism of authenticity and freedom.

"Oh, I had ways to keep my spirit alive," he said with a beautiful smile lifting his radiant seventy-six-year-old face. "My hut within the prison complex was detached from the main cells and was encircled with barbed-wire. I was indoors all the time, and the wire was a constant reminder of how precious freedom was. Like in the Buddha's teachings, obstacles can be seen as advantages; the loss of one's freedom can inspire the reflection on the preciousness of freedom. This filled me with joy.

"Also, I knew from my years as a practicing Buddhist monk the benefits of *sati* — mindfulness. Just do everything you do with awareness and there is no room in one's mind for negative thoughts. I approached every day in prison as I did as a monk in the monastery, mindfully. I tried to notice everything that occurred in my mind and body: everything you see, hear, taste, think, and smell becomes simply an experience, without anything extra placed upon it. Just phenomena. So in that way, too, the thought of imprisonment is seen as just a thought. It comes and goes. And without attachment to it there's no problem. It's just a thought. In this way I could keep my mind free of afflictive emotions.

"I would also regularly recite the Buddha's discourses as well as study them, which inspired me greatly.

"In addition, a small book containing quotations of Jesus was smuggled through to me. I very much liked his attitude of forgiveness and sincerity.

"Also, I made it a habit to give *dana* — the offering of a gift — to my jailers. I wanted to overcome any feelings of seeing them as the enemy so I tried to make it a practice of sharing a little of my food with them. They, too, had a hard life in prison. This eased my emotional and psychological pain to some extent.

"I abstained from taking food after midday," he continued. "There are many people in my country who are hungry due to the policies of this dictatorship. By not eating in the afternoon I remained in solidarity with them."

He paused and closed his eyes for a moment, then opened them, saying, "But most importantly I would reflect on the preciousness of my friendships. So in moments of difficulty I would envision their faces one by one and talk to them a bit. I would recall our moments of laughter and the joys we shared."

He then turned to me and held both my hands with his own, and with a warm tender smile said, "It's the love that you feel that keeps your sanity. It's the love that sets you free."

U Tin Oo's story reminds me of the importance of our shared presence, the necessity of bringing our very best qualities of being to the moments of our life — whether alone or in the company of others.

I ask myself as often as I need to: Can I renew my courage to love? Can I be in direct communion with myself, others, and the world, simultaneously? We are in this together. We need each other to actualize our full potential to love, our full potential to liberate ourselves and each other, together, as we evolve life into the future. From such an awakened state of presence we are free to live and die, while between them both we are ready to touch and be touched.

"Between you and me there is nothing but you and me."

~ **Vesna Krmpotic**

104.   TRUST

"*Trust* that the seeds of purification are within you.
Nurture them and you will awaken.
The form is useful, but it is awareness that liberates."

These were the final words of my teacher Sayadaw U Pandita to me on the day that I disrobed as a Buddhist monk and left the monastery in Burma in 1984.

"If he is indeed wise he does not bid you enter the house of his wisdom but rather lead you to the threshold of your own mind."

~ Kahil Gibran

105. THE LIGHT

"The test of the morality of a society is what it does for its children."

~ **Dietrich Bonhoeffer**

*A*ung *San Suu Kyi* reminds us that "the dream of a society ruled by loving kindness, reason and justice is a dream as old as civilized man.

Does it have to be an impossible dream?

Karl Popper, explaining his abiding optimism in so troubled a world as ours, said that 'the darkness had always been there but the light was new. Because it is new, it has to be tended with care and diligence.' It is true that even the smallest light cannot be extinguished by all the darkness in the world, because darkness is not wholly negative. It is merely an absence of light. But a small light cannot dispel acres of encircling gloom. It needs to grow stronger, to shed its brightness, further and further. And people need to accustom their eyes to the light to see it as a benediction rather than a pain and to learn to love it."

"I pray for all of us, oppressor and friend, that together we succeed in buildinga better world through human understanding and love, and that in doing so we may reduce the pain and suffering of all sentient beings."

~ **The 14th Dalai Lama**

106. CREATING THE FUTURE

"Nature is saying: This is it. Join me as partner," writes Jean Houston. "Deepen, not change so much but deepen, work on more levels and together we can take the changes and make them into transformation and not total collapse."

Am I optimistic?

*L*et Nelson Mandela answer that question. "I am fundamentally an optimist. Whether that comes from nature or nurture, I cannot say. Part of being optimistic is keeping one's head pointed toward the sun, one's feet moving forward. There were many dark moments when my faith in humanity was sorely tested, but I would not and could not give myself up to despair. That way lay defeat and death."

"We breathe the same air. The plants we eat become a part of us," Richard Trowbridge writes in his book *The Adventure of Creating the Future*. "The language invented by forgotten ancestors molds our mentality. The DNA that patterns us forms a living chain through time, and we are one link. The electrical and magnetic impulses that traverse the universe, the rain that falls on all things, unites us all in a single system. For long ages humans have allowed themselves to be separated by artificially dividing themselves according to parochial categories. Black. White. Muslim. Christian. Female. Male. Non-human. Human. Me. Them. These divisions are all creations of the mind. They were taken up long ago. They need to be rethought now that humanity has established global contact and has a more mature understanding of the

Earth's place in the universe, and the long ages of evolution we have all passed through together. Once enough people have attained an insight into the basic interrelatedness of all things, we will begin to heal the wounds caused by holding a view that we are separate from each other and from the earth."

And to keep "one's head pointed toward the sun" we must do as Thich Nhat Hanh, suggests, see "the practice of peace and reconciliation [as]...one of the most vital and artistic of human actions."

107. LOVING KINDNESS

"For small creatures such as we the vastness is bearable only through love."

~ **Carl Sagan**

In the spirit of life — co-creating a future to believe in — an offering: A meditation on illuminating the light of love.

*S*itting, or standing, walking or reclining, relaxed and comfortable, with eyes either open or closed, foster a feeling of love in your heart; feel it as a warm caring attitude towards oneself and others, like an inner sun shinning inwardly and outwardly in all directions; a feeling of love free of anxiety, fear, or ill will toward anyone.

With warmth ... send waves of love inwardly and outwardly, towards oneself and others.

A warmth radiating in all directions — far and near.

A warmth that remains firm and steady despite the vicissitudes of life.

A warmth radiating in all directions...silently repeating...

May my loved ones and my friends and family be joyful and free from suffering, conflict, and pain.

May my father and mother be joyful and free from suffering, conflict, and pain.

May my sisters, brothers, and relatives be joyful and free from suffering, conflict, and pain.

May everyone honor our inherent dependence
on each other and the environment.

May all animals and creatures and all forms
of life on earth live in safety and peace.

May I abide with a warm heart, clear mind,
and be free of suffering and pain.

May my daily activities contribute to the
contentment, healing and insights of others.

May I give peace to others and support the welfare of others.

May I have the courage to take risks for their well-being.

May all beings in the universe know happiness.

May all beings everywhere, in all dimensions
of the universe, know peace.

May all beings far and near, seen and
unseen, feel love and give love.

May all beings born and to be born, be
free of fear and suffering.

May all beings now and forever experience
their most liberating aspirations.

> "And what do all the great words come to in the end, but that?
> I love you, I am at rest with you, I have come home."
>
> ~ Dorothy Sayers

108.   OPENNESS

ACKNOWLEDGMENTS

For those of you, both alive and who have passed away, whose words and thoughts have been included in this book, I thank you from my heart for your generous contribution. May people everywhere benefit from your work and vision.

CONTACT ALAN CLEMENTS

contact@**WorldDharma**.com

WEB SITES

www.**AlanClements**.com

www.**WorldDharma**.com

STAY CONNECTED, SAY HELLO, VOLUNTEER, INTERN

Web developers, graphic artists, film & audio editors, social media mavericks, anyone who wants help out:

contact@**WorldDharma**.com

Join our e-mail list:

www.**WorldDharma**.com

AWAKENING WORLD DHARMA

The Art and Activism of Freedom
An Online Video Program with Alan Clements
based on "*A Future To Believe In.*"

www.**AFutureToBelieveIn**.com

www.**WorldDharmaInstitute**.com

ALSO BY ALAN CLEMENTS

*Burma: The Next Killing Fields?

"Alan Clements articulates the essentials of courage and leadership in a way that can stir people from all sectors of society into action; his voice is not only a great contribution during these changeful times, it is a needed one."

~ **Jack Healy, Former director of Amnesty International**

*Burma's Revolution of the Spirit: A Nation's Struggle for Freedom and Democracy (co-authored with Leslie Kean).

"Burma's Revolution of the Spirit is an outstanding photographic essay on a difficult and inspiring subject. It reflects with power and sensitivity the enduring beauty and the ongoing destruction in Burma, and the profound struggle of Aung San Suu Kyi, with all of Burma's peoples, for spiritual and democratic freedoms. Their struggle has great meaning for the human rights — and the humanity — of us all. We must each, in our own way, make the struggle our own."

~ **Representative Tom Lantos, United States Congress.**

The Voice of Hope — Conversations with Aung San Suu Kyi

"The Voice of Hope is a message that the world should hear."

~ **Former US President Jimmy Carter**

"Every leader on the planet should read this book at least once."

~ **Alice Walker, Pulitzer-Prize winning author of *The Color Purple***

"The dialogues in The Voice of Hope express Aung San Suu Kyi's humor, erudition, wisdom and accessibility, and demonstrate why she has become a world spiritual leader."

~ The New York Times Book Review

"Whatever the future of Burma, a possible future for politics itself is illuminated by these conversations."

~ The London Observer

Instinct for Freedom: Finding Liberation Through Living (also available in Spanish, Japanese, Turkish, and German.)

"During an era when a spate of shallow, narcissistic fiction has found a niche as 'sacred literature' Alan's work is a wonderful relief and reminder that the heart of spirituality still is, and will always be, compassion."

~ Bo Lozoff, Founder of the Prison Ashram Project and Human Kindness Foundation and author of We're All Doing Time and It's a Meaningful Life

"Rarely has a book touched me as deeply and personally as Instinct for Freedom. This profound work is a call to action, a spiritual force for change. May the beauty of Alan's writing and the power of his personal journey compel you to be true to your own heart so that we may all experience the gift of freedom in its purest form."

~ Cheryl Richardson, Author of Stand Up for Your Life

"This superbly written, profound, and moving work addresses head-on the central question of our time: how to put meditation into action and so transform the real conditions of the real world. Its honesty and passion are liberating, and its message both timeless and acutely timely."

~ Andrew Harvey, Author of The Direct Path and Sacred Activism

"Courageous and compelling, *Instinct for Freedom* is a vivid account of how one man's renunciation gave way to his own love and desire. This is a haunting and beautiful story, one full of teachings for seekers of all persuasions."

~ **Mark Epstein, M.D., Author of *Going to Pieces without Falling Apart***

"Alan is uniquely qualified to widen our perspectives, both of ourselves and of meaningful action in the world. His eloquence and sincerity calls us closer to our fullest potentials."

~ **Joseph Goldstein, Author of *One Dharma: The Emerging Western Buddhism***

ALAN CLEMENTS is an author, performing artist, media activist, and founder of the *World Dharma* vision. As the first American to ordain as a Buddhist monk in Burma, he lived for nearly five years in a Rangoon monastery training in Buddhist psychology and mindfulness meditation. In 1984 he was forced to leave the country by Burma's dictatorship, with no reason given. To the ire of the regime, he has returned numerous times to witness and document the human rights violations in that country. Subsequently, he has been "blacklisted" from reentering Burma by the military authorities.

Clements is the co-founder of the *Burma Project USA/ International*, a non-profit human rights and media advocacy organization dedicated to raising awareness of Burma's nonviolent struggle for freedom. He is also the co-founder of *The World Dharma Institute* (WDI), which offers an innovative video program exploring World Dharma — the art and activism of freedom. Inspired by Aung San Suu Kyi, Burma's Nobel Peace Laureate, the course finds its roots in Burma's nonviolent spiritual revolution and is based on Alan's latest book, *A Future to Believe In — 108 Reflections On The Art and Activism of Freedom.*

Clements is the author of *Burma: The Next Killing Fields?* (1991, with a foreword by the Dalai Lama). He is also the co-author with Leslie Kean and a contributing photographer to *Burma's Revolution of the Spirit* (1994, Aperture, NY) — a photographic tribute to Burma's struggle for democracy, with essays by eight Nobel Peace Laureates. In addition, Alan was the advisor and script revisor for *Beyond Rangoo*n (1995

Castle Rock Entertainment), a feature film depicting Burma's struggle for democracy, directed by John Boorman.

In 1996, Clements coauthored *The Voice of Hope*, the internationally acclaimed book of conversations with Aung San Suu Kyi, which moved Pulitzer-Prize winning author Alice Walker to write, "Every leader on the planet should read this book at least once."

Alan's additional book, *Instinct for Freedom — Finding Liberation through Living*, was nominated for the best spiritual teaching/ memoir by the National Spiritual Booksellers Association in 2003.

Clements is also a political/spiritual satirist, and performs *Spiritually Incorrect: In Defense of Being Human*, to audiences around the world, as benefits to raise awareness of Aung San Suu Kyi and her country's "revolution of the spirit."

Clements has been interviewed for NBC's Nightline, Global National, ABC Australia, CBC Canada, CBS Evening News, Talk to America, the New York Times, the Guardian, Newsweek and Time magazines, Conscious Living, Yoga Journal and numerous other media. In addition, he has presented to such organizations as Mikhail Gorbachev's State of The World Forum, The Soros Foundation, The United Nations Association of San Francisco, and delivered a keynote address at the John Ford Theater for Amnesty International's 30th year anniversary. Alan's web site is: **www.AlanClements.com**.

CPSIA information can be obtained at www.ICGtesting.com
Printed in the USA
LVOW120056260612

287654LV00007B/84/P